GOT YOUR SIX
A 12-MONTH JOURNAL FOR MILITARY SPOUSES

MEGAN CASPER
ALANA LE

GOT YOUR SIX: A 12-MONTH JOURNAL FOR MILITARY SPOUSES
Copyright © 2017 by Megan Casper and Alana Le
First Edition
All rights reserved.

No part of this book may be used or reproduced in any manner whatsoever without written permission except in the case of brief quotations embodied in critical articles or reviews.

For information contact:
hello@thesixbox.com

ISBN-13: 978-1976586187

CONTENTS

Introduction 1

How to Use this Journal 5

January: Goal Digger 6

February: Love Well 18

March: Spring Break 32

April: April Showers 40

May: We Remember 48

June: Summertime 56

July: You're Sizzlin' 64

August: Celebrate 72

September: At Ease 81

October: Contentment 93

November: Thankful for You 102

December: All I Want 112

Afterword 121

Acknowledgements 122

About the Authors 123

To the incredible military spouse, who laughs, cries, loves, and somehow always endures.

I guess a loving woman is indestructible.
—John Steinbeck

INTRODUCTION

Introduction

The girl sits alone on a bench outside. She clutches her phone in her hand and stares blankly at the wall opposite the bench. Inside, her friends laugh, talk, and smile widely, as though all is right with the world. She can't be around them right now, so she stepped out for some air, and now she can't seem to make herself go back inside.

Please, she thinks, *just one message. Just one word.* It's been so long since she last heard anything. Has something happened? She wills her phone to buzz, but it's silent. Her fingers itch to check the news one more time, but she refuses. What's the point? Whatever she discovers, there's nothing she can do.

Then that one dark thought enters her mind yet again: *What if they've been knocking on my door, and I missed it by being here? Should I go home?* They—the guys in uniform that no one wants to see. The ones who bring the worst news.

She stands abruptly and shoves her phone in her back pocket, then takes it out and holds it in her hand instead, just to make sure she doesn't miss a notification.

Back inside, she pastes a smile on her face. "This was so fun! Thank you for inviting me. I had *such* a great time!" Hugs, smiles, promises of future get-togethers. To the new acquaintances: "It was *so* great to meet you!"

The drive home is quiet and anxious. No radio. Just headlights and a death-grip on the steering wheel. She parks, but there's no one at the door after all.

Dinner at home, alone—a cold bowl of cereal, a silent phone. She charges the phone enough to last the night, then goes to bed with it clutched in her hand instead of plugged into the wall.

Buzz. She starts awake. She peers at her phone, squinting at the bright light from the screen. Is it him?

No. A friend from tonight. They must be just getting back home.

You okay? You were quiet tonight.

Tears begin to fall. She's so tired, and she's been on this rollercoaster for days. She wipes away the tears and replies: *Oh, I'm fine. Just a lot on my mind. Thanks for checking in! :)*

Because she can barely say the truth out loud, much less fire it off in a casual text to a friend—*actually, I'm desperately lonely and absolutely terrified that my husband is going to die.* No, that text definitely won't be getting sent.

The friend replies. *Glad to hear it. Let me know if you need anything!!*

Will do. But she knows she'll never ask them for anything. No one honestly wants to deal with her in this state, do they?

An hour later, she finally falls back asleep, then wakes disoriented at dawn, certain she just felt the phone buzz. No—still nothing. Another day on the rollercoaster begins.

She begins to wonder if she's invisible.

Invisible to the people who smile and say "How are you?" but never really want to know the answer. Invisible to her husband, the love of her life, who for some reason still hasn't contacted her. Invisible to the military who sent him out, to her friends, to her family. Invisible to the whole wide world.

Who is she?
We've both been that girl many times before. We're betting you have too.
She's the incredible, invisible military spouse.

Hold on, military spouse—you are *not* invisible

That girl's story is familiar, but it doesn't tell the whole truth. Not even close.

You are *not* truly invisible. Your service member sees you, loves you, and is incredibly grateful for you. Your family and friends care deeply about you. Your sacrifices are not meaningless, nor are they unseen.

Circumstances in this military life often align to make you feel invisible, putting you in situations where you can't talk about your fears, you're away from those who know you best, and you have no way to contact your spouse when they're gone. The distance, frequent moves, and all-consuming focus the military requires of families create a difficult dynamic where the people who love you do not often have the opportunity to tell you and show you how much you matter to them.

That doesn't change the fact that you *do* matter.

Military service takes a heavy toll on marriage

We know it's not always rainbows and roses being married to a member of the military.

Yes, there are incredible rewards and honor in the roles of both "service member" and "spouse of a service member," but there are also many moments

INTRODUCTION

of fear, uncertainty, loneliness and even heartache.

Deployments, moves, constant schedule changes, jobs that can't always be explained or even discussed—these all impact family life and marriage in intense, long-lasting ways.

Then you mix it all together and add in the honest-to-goodness fear and sadness that can creep in when the person you have chosen to do life with is sent to a location you have never seen and can't visit, and you aren't even sure what is happening in their day to day life. This heavy load can take an incredible toll on everyone.

Sometimes, it feels like being a military spouse could even be considered a calling.

While it takes a special sort of person, we also know firsthand it creates a special person.

You may not have known what you signed up for when you got started, but you learned fast and molded to the flexible, resilient and self-sacrificing spouse you were meant to be. (Of course, that process is easier when your spouse is appreciative, understanding, and communicates as much as they are able!)

During deployments, trainings, and busy times, you get in your groove and start to live more independently out of the need to survive and protect yourself from fear and pain.

You talk less or maybe you just share less as you don't want to burden or worry your partner. On top of a lack of connection we so often face in military relationships, military spouses can lose their sense of self, since their partner's career of service often takes precedence over theirs. Military spouses can have a harder time finding work than their partners and military couples can struggle to plan anything about their lives in advance (birthdays, holidays, anniversaries, etc.) which can continually test marriages and self-esteem. While many things can be turned into a positive, the struggle to work through the issues still remains.

Because marriage is work. And being married to the military can be even more work at times. We recognize that military spouses are not the only ones to have stress in their marriages, but the fact remains that the enlisted service member is still considered one of the most stressful jobs in America. The job puts the strain on everyone around them. We know both enlisted and officer wives who live stressful lives for different reasons, but often all equal in the level of stress.

All military marriages are unique in one particular way when compared to other relationships—you know right from the beginning that the military is first. They control where, when and how you live, when things are going to change and what that looks like.

In most other careers, you have some choice or you can say "no," but not so in the military. To borrow a favorite phrase from a friend, you "Suck it up, Buttercup" and make the most of it, no matter what the "it" is.

It is certainly not always easy being married to the military, but it *is* worth it

While military marriages can seem crazy stressful at times, they are incredibly rewarding when partners have tools to keep them going strong. Spouses and service members need to continually move towards each other to keep their relationship healthy and vibrant.

And military spouses in particular need to make a constant, intentional effort to remember the truth—they *are* significant and *not* invisible—in the face of the many lies, worries, and stresses that bombard them every day.

That's where this journal comes in.

HOW TO USE THIS JOURNAL

How to Use this Journal

This 12-month journal is a tool to help you work through the rollercoaster of high highs and low lows in military family life. Each month's theme is different, but always includes several writing prompts and a few pages of our own insights or lessons learned based on the theme.

Everything in this journal was developed based on our experiences as military spouses—the lonely nights, the lost dreams, the utterly overwhelming deployments, the pain of starting over every time a new group of friends moves on to the next duty station.

We poured our hearts into this monthly journal, because we know that while there are many organizations and resources available for military spouses who need support, no physical support, marriage retreat, or social event can completely heal a military spouse's heart. (No journal can either, of course—but it's a start!)

We need a way to process the tumultuous feelings that come along with military life, a way to record our dreams and our fears, and to keep moving forward and making plans even when it feels impossible.

At the start of each month, we suggest taking a few moments in a cozy chair with a warm cup of something yummy in hand to quietly read and evaluate the current theme. In each section, you will find content and prompts to help you think more deeply about a certain topic. You can tackle each month's writing prompts all at once, or save them to do once per week. The important thing is taking time for you to process and dream.

The months are not year-specific, so if you are starting this book in May, just begin with the month of May and come back to the early months of the year when you get there. That said, if a certain theme in a different month is standing out to you right now ... go for it! There is no right or wrong way to use this journal. We only hope that this journal helps you through the hard moments that will inevitably come this year, and that it gives you permission to dream, hope, and celebrate in the good moments.

January: Goal Digger

Little girls with dreams become women with vision.
-Unknown

Introduction

Do you ever step back and look at your life and think, "How did I get here?" Or do you look at a photo from a few years back and think, "Who was that crazy, carefree girl who just knew the world was her oyster?"

Tell us we aren't alone here.

While we have some physical goals (like adding in 15 minutes of working out each day—why does this always seem hard to do?), we want to also focus on the "heart" behind our goals. The reason behind our goals matters so much more than the goals themselves because it gives meaning and life to what we are hoping to accomplish.

We believe it is healthy to review where you have been *and* plan for where you want to go.

We know making "plans" as a military spouse often seems impossible as we know change will come this year. But being flexible and keeping a good attitude can be two additional goals for your list, right?

For January, we have included prompts to think deeper about your "why" behind your goals and also sections to write out your goals. There have been multiple studies that show people who write down goals have a much better chance of accomplishing them. We know the past year may not have been your best ever and you might be feeling discouraged or hesitant to even think about next year. We've been there. But we aren't giving up, and neither should you.

Let's focus this year on being a year of heart-filled goal setting that allows for grace and change. So here we go—let's write it out together and start the year off with some "goal digging"!

JANUARY: GOAL DIGGER

Looking Back

Last year may have been awesome for you personally or maybe for your family, or it may have been a year where getting out of bed each day was an accomplishment in and of itself. That's okay. Each year holds so many ups and downs in all areas of our lives. In the following pages, take some time to process the past year.

What happened last year that brought you joy?

GOT YOUR SIX

What did you struggle with last year? What do you wish you had done differently?

JANUARY: GOAL DIGGER

What moment are you most proud of from the past year? Describe the memory in detail—what happened, how it made you feel, and why it made you proud.

Your Hope

Remember yearbook signing in elementary school? The cliché "KIT" for keep in touch, "LYLAS" for love you like a sister, or "HAGS" for have a great summer—maybe we are just showing our age here. The end of the school year marked a feeling of accomplishment, a much-needed break and a chance to reset for next year.

We don't get these defined breaks very often as adults and often life can feel mundane or never changing. Let's view the end of the year as our "summer break"- a chance to review, reflect and refocus. You did it, you made it through the year, it's behind you now and you can re-focus on the new.

What do you hope the coming year brings in your life; in relationships, career, education, parenthood, finances or health?

JANUARY: GOAL DIGGER

Planning for Wiggle Room

One thing we don't want to do is hold on to "perfect" or "ideal" or "control"—got you with that last one, didn't we? It is so easy and tempting to want to think we can control life despite knowing we can't. Have you thought about how you react when challenges come your way? Have you tried hard to create a bubble or image so inflexible that when change, trials, and more come your way, you can't adapt and you freak out or shut down?

While we feel it is important to have a vision for your year and your life, we encourage you to build margin and room for the unexpected. Be sure your vision includes a woman who gives grace to others and herself, and whose life, emotions and heart, and doesn't totally implode when the inevitable changes come.

What are some ways you can alter your mindset to have a plan, but allow for wiggle room? This might be hard at first, but it will be worth it!

Core Goals

We've looked back at where we've been, written down hopes for the future, and thought about how we can become more flexible and open to change. Now it's time to think about core goals. We've broken the big picture down a bit to help get you started. We begin each section with a "heart" question, because we want you to keep in mind the purpose behind your goals.

Physical/Self: How can you care for yourself more?

Do you love to learn new things? Do you enjoy a weekly manicure? Do you need more time to read? Skype with a girlfriend or your mom? Do you need 15 minutes of pilates each day? What fills you up is important, because you can't pour from an empty cup.

Relationships: How can you foster stronger relationships?

Maybe you have always wanted to be better at sending cards regularly? Dropping cookies off at a friend's for no particular reason? Hiding love notes in your husband's pockets? Why do you value these ideas and what you hope they accomplish.

JANUARY: GOAL DIGGER

Aspirations/Dreams: Do you have a passion?

Do you have something you have always wanted to do or be better at? Or do you wish you had a special passion, but can't seem to figure it out? What do you feel you would gain by taking time to define or pursue these dreams?

Spiritual/Emotional: Do you give time to think about the deeper issues?

How much focus do you give this part of your life? Do you wish you spent more time doing so "digging deep" or maybe you need to spend less time "thinking" and more time "doing"? What books, people or events you can connect with that would help give you clarity?

Breaking Down Your Goals

As one of our high school English teachers always said, "It's easiest to eat an elephant one bite at a time." Oh, was she right.

You have your visions and goals in mind, but you know you can't do them immediately or even finish all of them this year, and that is okay. Break them into small chunks and tackle a little bit at a time.

Here are some of our recent small, broken-down goals:

- Each night set out coffee mug, book and journal so we can start fresh in the morning with time for ourselves.
- Wake up 30 minutes earlier than usual to read, plan and stretch for 10 minutes.
- On the first of each month, note who has a birthday or special day coming up and prep cards to send (we suggest purchasing a 12-month supply of cards to have on hand).
- Text a friend each Sunday night to see if they can get together for a walk, Skype date or chat that week.
- Secure a sitter for date night with your husband, schedule a lunch or coffee date on post with him.
- Schedule 15 minutes to work on a hobby each day or once a week, in a class, online, You Tube, or by having a friend help.

What are the small, daily, weekly, monthly steps you can take to make progress? Brainstorm here, then write these steps in your calendar now to make sure they are included in your life. You'll be amazed at how much progress you make over time.

JANUARY: GOAL DIGGER

You Can Do This

Whether this is your first time ever writing down goals or you do it every year, we are excited for you! Goal setting is a learned process and the more we do it, the better we get at it.

The main focus should be on *why* you want to do certain things as this will motivate you to keep going. Perhaps you want to eat better to have more energy for things you love, you want to read more to have greater wisdom and knowledge in life, you want to take a class in order to get a promotion or fulfill the dream of having your own business one day, etc.

Don't ignore the "why" behind goals, because that will make all the difference. Check in at the end of the year: Did you accomplish your goals? Did you decide to shift some goals for new or improved ones? Did your husband's deployment totally make you change course (ummm, we've been there)?

What aspect of goal setting comes easy to you?

Do you doubt that you can be successful with your goals? Why?

What are some things you can change to ensure this time will be different?

Food for Thought

Holding onto Your Dreams as a Military Spouse

We can feel a little weird talking about our dreams sometimes? It sounds like something a 4th grader would do, day dreaming of being a Superhero, the President of the United States or a Astronaut (or all three).

At the very least, dreaming feels like it belongs in someone else's life—someone with more opportunities and unlimited resources; someone who doesn't have all of the obligations, stresses, and responsibilities that come along with being a military spouse.

And it's true, most of us will never accomplish the exact dreams we had as a 4th grader, or even as a high school student. As military spouses, we've chosen a path that requires insane amounts of self-sacrifice, and for many of us that has included giving up some of our most cherished dreams.

But does that mean a military spouse has to give up on dreams completely? We don't think so!!

Here are a few of our learned-the-hard-way tips for holding onto your dreams as a military spouse:

Let your dreams evolve

Come back to that 4th grade dream: What did you think you would be or achieve as an adult? Let us guess … those dreams were eventually set aside for something else, right?

There's nothing wrong with turning from one dream to a new one, or letting a dream evolve into something slightly different that makes more sense.

In fact, isn't it healthier to be perceptive to changes in your own life and to the world around you and shift accordingly, rather than holding single-mindedly to your original plan?

Put dreams in their place

Military spouses often feel like we only have two choices—either give up our own dreams and put the military and the service member's career first, or put our own dreams first no matter what the cost to our marriage and our family.

This is such an unhelpful feeling, isn't it? It makes us feel trapped and judged at every turn, like there's never going to be a good answer for us.

But it just isn't true. There are way more than two choices out there—there are millions of choices! The right choice for you and your family may depend on a multitude of different factors, and may be different in every new season of life.

What we've found is the key is to put your dreams in their place. In other words, don't let them rule the top spot of your priority list when you have other priorities too.

JANUARY: GOAL DIGGER

If a dream is making you feel trapped, pressured, stressed out, and unhappy, then maybe it's time for that dream to change.

If you and your family are paying too high a price for that dream, it's okay to admit it and change your mind.

After all, if we're dominated by our dreams and driven to pursue them at any cost, that can be the same degree of tyranny as not being able to dream at all.

Dream big, but start small

Set goals in the context of where you are coming from and where you want to be going in the long term. How will each of your goals contribute to what you want your life to be like when you are 80 years old?

This approach helps connect the dots and realize how the small things we do every day and week contribute to our big dreams.

For example, if we want to leave a financial legacy for the next generation in our family, that starts today with sticking to the budget, saying "no" to that extra latte or new outfit, paying off debt, etc. The small daily sacrifices have greater meaning because we've started seeing how important they are in the big picture.

We think this perspective is helpful for military spouses too. We are often too scared to dream big because it feels so impossible that we will ever be able to achieve those dreams.

But sometimes all we need is to start taking little, baby steps in the direction of those dreams.

It might take 5, 10, even 20 years or more to reach them, and we might learn something new and change our minds along the way.

But the important thing is to keep dreaming, keep moving, and keep trying, even if it's just in small ways that fit into the current margins of our lives.

Every accomplishment starts with the decision to try.
—JFK

February: Love Well

Introduction

The greatest thing you'll ever learn is just to love and be loved in return.
—Nat King Cole

Does it ever feel like we say "love" so much that it's lost some meaning? "I love Starbucks," "I love vacation," "I love my job" (okay, you don't hear that last one a lot). Love is such a powerful word used in so many ways, but often in a more flippant manner, which is why this month we are focusing on ways we can define and take action on "loving well."

Love doesn't have to be only romantic. It can be shown towards a friend, a family member, a stranger, the planet or more. There are many ways to express love and just as many ways to receive it too. There are moments when a small gesture is all that is needed and other times when something grander is called for.

This month, we have included common ways people give and receive love along with ideas on how to express love in each way.

We know love might be a painful topic for you as your marriage might be struggling during a deployment or you're just dealing with the heartache of having your partner away. Showing love may be a challenge, but we believe these ideas and small steps could help in your journey just the same.

Let's choose to love well together and see what happens in our hearts or the hearts of those we touch by the end of February!

FEBRUARY: LOVE WELL

Know Yourself

We all feel loved in different ways. When was the last time you really felt loved on (either by your spouse, friends, family, co-workers, etc.)? For example, do you really appreciate when people physically do things for you, give gifts, drop off a meal, plan a special event or do something "just because?"

Write down a few memories of a time you felt loved. Notice any trends?

Loving Well

We came across an article that described a woman who used to love people "like a rolling pin"—shaping and forming as she went. Ouch! How many times have we shown "love" in hopes of forming or controlling someone else? This is one of the reasons why we want to focus on loving well this month—loving without expectation, loving someone right where they are today.

Love cannot be rushed or forced. It has to be given the space to grow and breathe. Here are some more thoughts about love:

- To love well is to refuse to let someone's imperfections define them.
- Loving well is all about giving people the time and space they need as they grow.
- To love well is to know when to stop talking and just listen.
- To love well is to show more gratitude than disappointment.
- Love finds peace in the chaos.
- To love well is to look for ways to be an encourager.
- Love is a choice, not just a feeling.

Which of those truths resonates most with you? Why do you think that is the case?

FEBRUARY: LOVE WELL

Your Love Story

Perhaps someone in your life has been a great example of love to you—many times we think of our parents, who sacrifice so much for us. Maybe you didn't have parents who were the best examples, but friends, other family members, neighbors and even spouses can fill in those gaps in life. Maybe your view of love even changed after reading a book or watching a powerful film. You might even be in a phase of life where your view of love is evolving. Regardless of where you are right now, you have a love story—a story of your experience with love.

How would you define love?

Who has been the most positive example in your life of love?

What do you wish you had known about loving others when you were younger?

GOT YOUR SIX

Ways to Love

Gary Chapman wrote a well-known book called *The 5 Love Languages* where he breaks down what he believes are the main ways people give and receive love. We highly recommend it, if you haven't read it already. The book is very practical and most people do identify with one or more of the five ways he describes love in the book. We have offered some ideas on the following pages to help you figure out how you best like to give and receive love.

Read through the "love languages" we've outlined on the following pages first, then come back to this question. Or, if you already know your love language, go ahead and take note of it now.

Which love languages speak the most to you? What do you think your spouse's love language is?

FEBRUARY: LOVE WELL
Words of Affirmation

Are you the kind of person who enjoys receiving cards, texts, emails, or snail mail? Do you save cards and notes people have given you over the years? Do you feel more motivated when someone compliments you? Words just might be your love language.

Here are some ways to show love with words:
- Send a card.
- Sneak post-it notes with sweet messages into someone's suitcase, lunch or uniform to find later.
- Intentionally saying what you think or feel about someone.
- Keep a journal for a few months where you write down all the things you love or appreciate about someone and then gift it to them.

What are more ways you can show love with words of affirmation?

Who do you feel would appreciate your words?

GOT YOUR SIX

Acts of Service

Do you feel totally amazed when someone helps you around the house, washes your car, or drives you to the airport? Do you love coming downstairs and seeing the dishes have been washed and put away? This might be your language then!

Here are some ways to show love with service:
- Babysit for free.
- Bring food over to someone's home when you know they are sick.
- Walk someone's dog when you know they are busy.
- Share a car if someone needs transportation.
- Salt someone's driveway before a snow storm (our neighbors did this when our husbands were gone and just texted after the fact, so we didn't even know it was happening!)
- Do the dishes or laundry for your spouse.

What are more ways you can show love with acts of service?

Who do you feel would appreciate your service?

FEBRUARY: LOVE WELL

Receiving Gifts

Do you love jewelry (this is not a trick question)? Do you feel loved when your husband shows up with flowers? Do you get excited when your mom asks what you want for your birthday? Maybe your love language is gifts—no shame!

Here are some ways to show love with gifts:
- Purchase an item for someone they want, but doesn't need.
- Bring back something fun from vacation for a friend (one time a dear friend mailed Megan a coconut!)
- Make someone their favorite dessert (service + gift in our book!)
- Take family photos for free for a friend you know whose husband is preparing to deploy.
- Give a give a gift card for a special dinner to a friend who is preparing to welcome home her husband.

What are more ways to show love with receiving gifts?

Who do you feel would appreciate gifts from you?

GOT YOUR SIX
Quality Time

This one is hard for the military spouse, isn't it? Living thousands of miles from your spouse or family makes it hard to fulfill if this is you. Do you feel not only lonely, but desire time via phone, text or in person with your spouse and dear friends? Or maybe even humans in general if you are on your own or in a new place? Your love language might be quality time.

Here are some ways to show love with quality time:
- Schedule Skype/FaceTime chats regularly.
- Join an interest group where you meet up in person with a group.
- If you are local, then plan coffee dates, monthly girl's nights or kid play dates with friends.
- When you spouse is home, plan time to hang out, undistracted.
- Invite someone to join you for a movie, museum visit or road trip.

What are more ways to show love with quality time?

Who do you feel would appreciate your time?

FEBRUARY: LOVE WELL

Physical Touch

Anyone can have this love language and it doesn't mean just the sexy kind. Do you love hugs? Do you enjoy foot rubs? Do you love it when your husband sits next to you in a room full of people or in the same booth at a restaurant? Do you find yourself always wanting to hold hands? Then this might be you!

Here are some ways to show love with quality time:
- Hold hands.
- Offer a back massage or even a gift card to get a pedicure.
- Give big, genuine hugs to those you love.
- Give high fives.
- Put your arm around someone (someone you know, of course).
- Sit with someone who looks a little lonely.

What are more ways to show love with physical touch?

Who do you feel would appreciate a hug, high five or maybe gift card for a massage?

Filling the Tank

Perhaps you've seen firsthand what it looks like when two people have very different love languages and don't always fill each other's "love tanks." Growing up, maybe you remember your dad was always offering to fix a car, drive someone somewhere, help out with dishes—he served. He wasn't much for words or gifts, which tended to be your mom's love languages—ahh, see the problem already? It takes real effort when you have different languages and even more effort if your spouse or family live thousands of miles from you!

Think about how you feel loved and what ways you find it easiest to show love, then compare notes with your spouse or friends. You can just even ask them, "When was a time you felt most loved by me?"

It is important to both have your tank filled and fill others' tanks.

How can you make sure your own tank is filled? Brainstorm a few ways to let others around you know what makes you feel loved:

Write down other ideas you have about filling others' tanks with love, even if it means stepping outside the comfort zone of your primary love language:

FEBRUARY: LOVE WELL

Receiving Love

Letting someone love you ... this one can be hardest of all, can't it? We military spouses run around ensuring so many other people's needs are met that we often let our own tanks run dry. We confess we are guilty of doing this to ourselves—running food to a neighbor, serving at an FRG event, cleaning up after our families, making awesome care packages for service members, but when someone asks what they can do to help us, we simply say, "I'm fine, I've got this." It can even feel like "weakness" to accept love at times.

We challenge you not to let this happen. Be open to others wanting to serve and love on you. You cannot run around filling up everyone else if you yourself are not filled. If your husband offers to watch the kids so you can get a mani/pedi or have some wine and a bubble bath—let him! If your mother-in-law comes in town and offers to cook—let her! If your friend drops by when your house is messy and says, "Let's go somewhere fun," or "Can I come hang out?"—just take her up on it! If your husband tries to Skype in the middle of dinner it feels like a bad time, but really, you can delay dinner and spend an extra 15 minutes chatting with him—do it!

Sometimes we might not even recognize that someone is attempting to love on us. This month keep your eyes and ears open and let people in, no matter how scary or "weak" it might feel.

What are some reasons you find it hard to receive love? Why do you feel it is challenging for you?

GOT YOUR SIX

Food for Thought

Love Letter: Deployment and My Daughter

Megan welcomed her husband home from deployment and a new baby boy into the world within hours of each other in 2017. Before all the craziness happened, she drafted this beautiful love letter to her (at the time) almost-two-year-old daughter:

Dear Daughter,

It's been just me and you for a few months now. Last May, the month Daddy left, I was so scared, worried and anxious when we first started down this road. The road where I thought, "This might be the last time I see my husband," and "How do people make it through this?" I look back at photos of sweet little 14-month-old you and realize you didn't smile or laugh once the day he left. I think you could tell that something big was happening. It's incredible what little ones pick up on.

We stood under the large awning covering a cold, concrete courtyard where your Daddy's office buildings surrounded us, nervously laughing with other spouses, parents, girlfriends and kids. We tried to pay attention to the Commander's speech before the buses pulled up, but we all knew the ceremony meant the time to say goodbye was next. How can you fully pay attention to conversations around you when all you can think about is, "Is this really the last time my family will all be together until next year or forever?" Or, "This is the last time we will ever be together just as we are right now," because deep down you know anything can happen in a deployment. You will experience things you didn't expect, grow and change in ways you didn't mean to and then have to learn to fall together again after so much has happened.

Recently, a friend confessed to me they had never thought of the fact that "homecoming" might be hard. That each person in the family had changed. Reintegration it isn't always cupcakes, roses and sunshine. Sometimes it's cold shoulders, feeling far away still despite standing next to each other, long nights, hard days and more. One more thing to add to our list of worries.

It wasn't easy while Daddy was gone. I sat up more nights worrying about fevers, coughs and "it's-2am-what-do-I-do-if-something-really-is-wrong?" more times than I imagined. Oh, I wanted your Daddy there to sit with me and calm me down, but I learned to move through it (and eventually, not Google every single symptom).

I checked and re-checked that bills were paid, things around the house were taken care of, the car was in good shape, we were eating

FEBRUARY: LOVE WELL

somewhat decent meals, the dog went out, I was staying on top of work and more. All while also worrying about your Daddy.

You were 14 months when he left and you will turn 2 years old a couple weeks after he comes home. And what a chatty, independent and funny almost 2-year-old you've become. I am learning more about you, your sassy ways and sneaky grins, when you are scared, embarrassed, nervous, or just need a hug. I know when you are playing around and when you really are struggling or acting out. Your Daddy will have to learn these things about you too.

Sweet daughter, we have learned to lean on each other, even though you are so small. If you think Mama is sad or worried you quickly offer an "It's okay, Mama," and a pat or laying of your head on my shoulder. My tenderhearted girl who is already learning how to comfort and nurture before the age of 2. I've seen you try to be strong and hold back worry if you think your Mama is worried. You are so brave, just like the other military kids around you who learn at so young an age to be brave.

I didn't always get it right over these past few months. I wasn't always patient, strong, or motivated. But I never held back love. I never held back holding you when you were sad or sick. I never wanted you to think you were without a parent who loves you more than life itself.

Being your Mama has changed me. Being your Mama without Daddy around (while worrying about him) has changed me. I know he will have to adjust to that when he comes home, just as I will have to adjust to "sharing" you with him again. It won't just be me and you on the couch on Friday nights, won't be just us going for walk to the park, to our favorite coffee shop to share a cookie, or walking around aimlessly around Target looking at toys. But it also just won't be me and you when we are sick, tired, scared, worried, stressed or even happy. We will have someone to share in our sorrows or with us and we can't wait!

Here we are now, at the end. And guess what little one? We made it.

I am so excited to see your Daddy's face when he sees what a big girl you are, hear him laughing at your silly stories and songs, rock you to sleep at night and take you on special Daddy/Daughter adventures.

We are excited for homecoming and a little anxious too, if we are honest. We will be learning about each other again after months apart and it will require more bravery and bring new unknowns. More than anything, we want you to know you have a Mommy and Daddy who love you more than you will ever know, no matter where we are called to be in the world.

We are so excited for his return home! We know Daddy can't wait to kiss you each night before bed and hug you each morning!

Love,
Mama

March: Spring Break

Introduction

Almost anything will work again if you unplug it a for a few minutes, including you.
—Anne Lamott

Oh, the memories of spring break! Growing up, you may have looked forward to the break in the long school year—a time to refresh, take it easy, and hopefully enjoy some sunshine. As we get older, we forget to take breaks for ourselves, don't we? We start to think of "spring break" as either a burden or chore—a week we need to fill with activity for our kids or if you are still in school, maybe you just want to lay around the house instead of going on any adventure.

Perhaps spring break doesn't conjure up happy memories for you or it just means more of winter until April or May arrive. We challenge you to change your view this month and take a real break.

Spring officially begins on March 20th and while it may not mean sunshine and cruises for you, it can still mean a time of refreshment.

This month we wanted to inspire you to find ways to give yourself a real break.

MARCH: SPRING BREAK

Take a Load Off

We are somehow three months into the year already. Let's take a brief pause and evaluate how things are going so far.

Are you burning through your goals? Have you stuck with your workout routine? Are you getting the support you need and want from home or friends/family members?

Or does this year sort of stink so far? Maybe you didn't even set goals (nothing wrong with that). Maybe you fell off the wagon pretty fast or you just didn't get the support you needed to get started. Possibly, you PCS'd suddenly or your partner received orders unexpectedly. All of these things and more can knock a girl off her feet pretty fast.

Time to get real. Where are you at in life right now? Vent or celebrate in the space below:

Give Yourself a Break

We are admittedly women who love goals, challenging ourselves and maintaining running to do lists. (C'mon, we started The Six Box in the midst of raising toddlers, full time "day careers" and with husbands who were deployed or in training.) However, it also sounds like we love burning the candle at both ends.

But we have learned the hard way that while it can be difficult to take a break when we need one, it is so necessary. As military spouses, no matter what you have going on in life, it can be hard to give yourself permission to take a break. Thirty minutes can feel like a luxury and sometimes the "break" you are taking is really just writing a to do list or doing something that isn't actually restful to you.

Do you give yourself permission to take breaks? Why or why not?

What do you think needs so you aren't heading to "burn out mode?"

MARCH: SPRING BREAK

Break from Guilt

Let's agree to stop feeling guilty about taking a break right now, deal? Whether it's five deep breaths, a bubble bath and a good book, a walk (alone) around the neighborhood or just the yard, or maybe a monthly massage, take the break!

It's not that you just deserve it (side note, you do), it's that you are better for it. *You cannot pour from an empty cup.*

Now that we have given you permission, what will you tell yourself (and anyone else who asks why) the next time you feel you need a break and second guess it? Write it down here:

*Health is the greatest possession.
Contentment is the greatest treasure.
Confidence is the greatest friend.
—Lao Tzu*

Break Me Off Some of That

What is your happy place? If you could have an entire day of rest what would it look like? A day at the beach—salty toes, wind-blown hair, waves lapping near your chair, warm sun on your skin and someone else bringing you a fresh margarita ... okay, we better stop or we will buy the plane ticket to Mexico without talking to anyone else first.

Maybe you need a week at the beach, or a day, or just 2 hours on a lawn chair in the front yard (hey, neighbors!) On the other hand, we know that just might not be a possibility right now, but maybe a pedicure is (it's kind of like waves lapping at your chair, right?) Or maybe a morning at your local coffee shop alone is enough to recharge you. Maybe a girl's night is what you need. Maybe a yoga class. Maybe snuggling puppies at a shelter.

Make a list below of things that sound truly relaxing to you. Keep this list close by so the next time you find yourself with time, you know exactly how you will spend it.

MARCH: SPRING BREAK

Let It Go

Taking breaks is important and giving yourself permission to take them is even more important. We know you are most likely in the midst of a deployment, PCS move, time of loneliness in this military journey (if we are honest, a lot of military life is lonely). We understand. We have been there. We bet we could really laugh over some of the ridiculousness of military life together, ups and downs, changing orders, goodbyes and reunions which are so hard, and then of course the good ol' deployment "gnome" that is totally real. Everything always breaks at once when our husbands leave.

We say this to remind you that you aren't alone. You need a break. You deserve a break. You aren't superwoman and you don't need to pretend to be her. Ask for help. Toss the to do list. Watch Parks and Rec with some red wine. Drop the kids off at hourly care while you go to Target.

Take. A. Break.

The worst thing you could do is keep going until you break down. Self-care just as important as caring for everyone else so make sure you do it.

How are you going to take a "Spring Break" this month? Write down a specific plan:

Are you going to invite anyone to join you or do you need time by yourself?

GOT YOUR SIX

Food for Thought

Take a Time Out

Can we just say that sometimes military family life gets way out of control?!

You have the inevitable deployment looming on the horizon. The training trips leading up to it. The long hours your spouse puts in at work when they actually are home.

Then it always seems to coincide with a speed bump in your career, or complications in your pregnancy, or family emergencies, sickness, teething babies, and more.

Because it's not enough to deal with the many struggles and challenges of regular adult life. We had to add in military life as well.

For many of us maybe taking a whole or half day off just isn't possible right now—we are solo parenting and living far away from family members who might help us take a break, or we're working, going to school, and more. And we all have real life responsibilities. Those things don't just conveniently go away when we are stressed and need a break.

So, if a real break is not an option for you this month … how about a "time out"?

Read on for our ideas on ways to take a small physical, mental, or emotional "time out." These might seem small, but in our experience, taking little breaks goes a long way toward preserving our sanity and preventing burn-out.

Physical Time Out:

- Ask someone to clean the house.
- Pay someone to clean your car.
- Ride your bike around and get some fresh air.
- Take a long walk outside, taking in nature.
- Sit on the couch and watch a funny show.
- Read a book in a coffee shop.
- Leave the laundry for another day.
- Order pizza (don't cook or do dishes).
- Make a doctor's appointment—seriously, how often do we put our physical selves behind everyone else?
- Take a nap.

Mental Time Out:

- Don't look at your to-do list today.
- Put your phone far away from you so you aren't tempted to scroll through social media feeds, compare, or waste valuable rest time.
- Tell yourself things you like about you (do not criticize).
- Write a friendly note to a friend or family member.

MARCH: SPRING BREAK

- Light a candle you enjoy and savor the scent.
- Watch one episode of a funny show (not a mindless binge).
- Take a nap.

Emotional Time Out:

- Call a friend who makes you laugh.
- Hang out with a friend and agree to relax (not complain or stress together over life).
- Sometimes you can get worked up hearing about someone else's situation, so be careful to surround yourself with positivity right now.
- Yep, here we go again: take a nap! Your brain, heart and body need sleep.

April: April Showers

Introduction

Sweet April showers do bring May flowers.
—Thomas Tusser

Spring can be such a beautiful time of year (even in our very rainy Washington State). If you live in a cold and rainy spot like we do, spring is often when people come out of their homes—to socialize, exercise or bask in daylight!

However, we are just at the start of seeing the changes—still battling the gloomy, rainy days, with the sun setting earlier than we would like, and dealing with the overall sluggish feeling that this season still clings to. We know life can be this way sometimes too. You just can't seem to break through the clouds and fog to the light. We have been there and in the past year have experienced our own clouds—husbands gone, saying goodbye to friends, financial surprises, sickness after sickness in our houses, and job disappointments.

Life isn't always sunny. Sometimes you are stuck in a rainy season for a while and it feels like true Spring—you know, the whole "May Flowers" part—just never comes. Military spouses deal with so many uncertainties, unique challenges, and stressors that a large majority of our non-military friends just never will deal with.

This month, let's look at these very real stressors and work to find ways to prepare for them or change perspective when they come. We are walking this road together and are so thankful for the military spouse community that keeps us encouraged and comforted during those hard times.

APRIL: APRIL SHOWERS

Your April Showers

We have all experienced hard times as military spouses, sometimes even the same issue over and over again. If you are a new military spouse you might not have experienced too many yet or any at all, but you will.

We have come to learn that it is good and healing to acknowledge these hard times and anxiety-inducing situations. We encourage you to do the same.

Here are a few things we have each dealt with or seen friends go through. Circle or underline ones you can relate to right now:

- Deployment
- Multiple PCS moves (including cross country and out of country)
- Financial limitations or surprises
- Children with health or developmental issues
- PTSD
- Loneliness
- Uncertainty
- Unemployment or feeling unfulfilled in a job (especially due to frequent moving)
- Comparison to other military spouses
- Parenting struggles during deployment or reintegration
- Lack of/or poor communication with spouse
- Self-image struggles
- Disliking new duty station
- Drama or lack of support from other military spouses
- Family/friends not understanding military life/career demands

What additional "April Showers" might you be experiencing right now?

Root of the Rain

At first it might seem obvious where the rain showers in your life come from, but so often the rain and intensity of the storm started from a small habit, thought or moment that we didn't see at first.

Looking at any of the particular storms you are currently dealing with or have dealt with, do you see where they originated? A fear? A careless comment? A betrayal? Your own bad habit or attitude?

APRIL: APRIL SHOWERS

Storms are Brewing

We can promise you something right now—Spring comes every year, like clockwork. The rain comes down, the puddles appear, and you need to prepare. Get out the boots, the umbrella or just resign yourself to keep doing your regular activities a little wetter than usual (like we do in the Pacific Northwest).

Maybe living out in Washington has taught us a thing or two about continuing to move forward despite the rain, but really, we think it was becoming military spouses. Military spouses are pros at continuing forward despite the storms, aren't we? Which isn't always a bad thing. It's dangerous to wait like a sitting duck when signs of trouble are brewing. It helps to prepare physically and mentally.

When you sense trouble coming, how do you prepare?

Do you shut down, curl up and pull the covers over your head? Do you overcompensate with a fake smile and positive comments to everyone around you? Or do you hang somewhere in the middle, recognizing this is a rough patch and you aren't sure what to do, but you know you need to work through it?

What patterns do you see in your life in how you deal with hard times? Is there anything you feel needs to change?

Putting on Your Raincoat

In the previous section, you wrote down some ways that you see yourself trying to cope with the hard seasons that come up in military life. Here, we're sharing some of our own survival tactics, with space beneath each one.

Use the blank space to write down ways you might want to use each strategy in your own April showers this year.

Journaling

It can be so helpful for us when we get our thoughts and struggles out on paper and see them more objectively. Journaling also allows us to identify unhelpful or unrealistic thinking ("My spouse always puts work before our family!") and replace it with more constructive thoughts ("My spouse is going through a busy season at work, but I know it won't last forever.)"

Stepping down from extra commitments

One thing we've realized is that we tend to over-commit. Sometimes, everything works out, and we're tired, but proud of all we've accomplished. Other times, the packed schedules and hectic days are an unnecessary burden, and that's especially true when we're going through a period of rain showers in military life, whether it's a busy time at work or a deployment or something else. Stepping down from extra commitments helps us make sure we have the time and energy we need to keep doing the things that matter most during a rainy season.

APRIL: APRIL SHOWERS

Stepping up other kinds of commitments

Conversely, sometimes it helps to be more outward-focused in a hard season. Baking surprise cupcakes for a friend or inviting someone you've missed over for coffee can give you both a pick-me-up, and it is not as time-consuming as a regular volunteer position or weekly meeting.

Organizing local day or weekend trips

Scheduling trips to explore your local area can help if you're getting to know a new duty station, but it can also help give you something to look forward to in the midst of stress. A change of scenery often refreshes us, so that when we come back, we have more energy and creativity to bring to our day-to-day lives.

Setting reasonable goals

Finally, we find it helps to make sure the goals we've set for ourselves are reasonable if we know a metaphorical rainy season is coming. We still set goals—we love goals—but we make them smaller, or focus mainly on one particular area, rather than the long list of goals we might have if life were easier right now.

Rainbows and Roses

Here are two things we love about the rain: 1) Sometimes, it coincides with sunshine to create beautiful rainbows; and 2) It provides needed moisture so thirsty flowers can grow. Can you find some things to love about the rain showers in your life right now?

What are you grateful for even in this rainy season? Bonus points if you can find a few things that have been unexpected by-products of the hardships you've been going through.

APRIL: APRIL SHOWERS

Food for Thought

Share the Love

The year 2017 at JBLM brought a record amount of rain—44 inches, the most in that period since 1895.

It drove us nuts, kept us indoors with high-energy toddlers, and foiled our plans to run, hike, walk, and wear cute sunny-weather outfits. It's supposed to be spring, right?! Why were we all still wearing leggings and rain boots?!

But as frustrating as the weather was, we also knew that sunshine was on the horizon. We held on to the truth that the rain doesn't last forever.

No matter what frustrating rain showers you might be experiencing right now, a day *will* come when they *will* end. The sun will shine brightly again and circumstances will change, maybe not always in the way you expect, but we believe there are sunny days ahead for you. And when that day comes, we will be celebrating with you. But we'd also like to give you a challenge:

When your current rainy season finally ends, will you look around for others who are still stuck in a seemingly never-ending rainy season?

And will you think of ways to actively reach out and share your "spring flowers"—that is, share some of your own abundance with those who are in need of encouragement?

You might have more free time once your spouse gets home. What if you use some of it to make meals for a friend whose spouse is still deployed?

Or you might find yourself in a sunny, optimistic mood once things are going well for you at work. What if you put that happy mood to work and write a note of encouragement for someone who needs to know how valuable and important they are to you?

Part of the joy of entering a new, less-stressful season is being able to share what you have, now that you're not in "survival mode" anymore. So, next time you get to see the sun break through the clouds of your life, use the opportunity to look around for someone else who needs a bit of sunshine.

Being a military spouse can be isolating and challenging. *Good thing we don't have to do it alone.*

May: We Remember

Introduction

If silence was ever golden, it must be beside these graves.
—James A. Garfield

Memorial Day holds a deeper meaning to those of us who are part of military families.

Perhaps we take it so seriously because we have been directly impacted. We either know the ultimate sacrifice first hand, we have watched others experience it, or we know the real feeling of fear that this could be the last goodbye when we wave to our service members as they board the buses, planes and ships to serve our country.

While we can still enjoy the hotdogs, pool parties and start to summer Memorial Day is for so many, this month we wanted to pause and honor those who have paid it all.

We encourage you to look for a few quiet moments this month and spend time reflecting on what Memorial Day means in the pages of this journal and in the actions of your life.

MAY: WE REMEMBER

Telling Stories

Many of us come from military families or have been one for a long time. One of the greatest ways to honor those who have fallen, or to honor those who serve in general, is by telling their story.

Take a few moments to write your family's story. Did your grandfather serve on the front lines? Was your great aunt a nurse in a military hospital? Is your father a vet? Have you personally served in the military?

GOT YOUR SIX

What has been the story of your own spouse's military service so far?

MAY: WE REMEMBER

Have you experienced the loss of a close family member or friend? How do these stories affect your life?

GOT YOUR SIX

How Do You Persevere?

As a military spouse, you serve and sacrifice in ways that sometime seem unnoticed, small, and insignificant. But trust us when we say that your sacrifices are none of those things. Your hard work, prayers, and willingness to keep smiling and saying goodbye as many times as you have to—these are powerful, awe-inspiring things.

What has been the story of *your* sacrifices as a military spouse?

What motivates you to keep going even when things feel impossibly hard?

MAY: WE REMEMBER

Honoring in Living

We believe military spouses are in a unique and influential position to remember and honor the sacrifices of those who have given their lives for our country, since as spouses, we often stand as a bridge between the civilian and military communities.

Perhaps you personally know what it's like to wonder if this is your last kiss, or have found yourself praying desperate prayers you never thought you'd utter—prayers like "Please, Lord, no IED's." Or maybe you've carried your phone everywhere with you for 9 months, checking it a thousand times a day, just hoping for a text or call—anything to know your service member is okay.

Maybe you've lost friends who gave their lives in military service, or you know a Gold Star Spouse and you've seen their sacrifice and pain firsthand.

Memorial Day is so much more than a day of discounts and barbecues. It's a day of honoring and remembering those who have sacrificed their very lives so that we could live in safety and freedom.

But what can you actually do to honor those lives that have been lost? One of the greatest ways we can honor those who have paid the ultimate sacrifice is in how we live our lives. We think of it as "honoring by living."

This could take the form of getting involved with one of the many organizations that are active in honoring fallen soldiers and caring for their families. A personal favorite of ours is Wear Blue: Run to Remember, but there are many more that are worth getting to know.

Do some research and make a plan: what will you do to honor the sacrifices of fallen soldiers this Memorial Day?

Food for Thought

Five Ways to be a Bridge Between the Military and Civilians

Today, more than ever, the drift between "military" and "civilian" is growing. Less than 1% of our country serves in the Armed Forces compared to a high of 12% during WWII and 8% during Vietnam. Most of what Americans know about the military is based on movies and television shows which, as we all know, often do not accurately portray the daily life of service members and their families.

Since almost 99% of our country has limited to no experience with military life, it's inevitable that a disconnect has arisen between what is believed about those who serve versus what they actually do. This is particularly obvious on holidays such as Memorial Day and Veterans Day, when you often see people getting the meanings confused. While missing the meanings is not intentional, it is more a result of lack of knowledge or familiarity with military service, it does increase the distance felt between service members and civilians. One encouraging thing we see in today's society is the overall sense of respect for those who wear the uniform, so while the misunderstanding can be hurtful, the desire to support our military is there.

While civilians can do more to connect with service members and families, military spouses can be a powerful bridge to help others understand military service more. They are in a unique position to understand and advocate on behalf of their spouse and family, while also communicating with civilians about their unique struggles and wins. While military spouses are serving their country, they can sometimes be seen as someone who understands both sides due to the fact that they aren't physically "wearing the uniform." Here are five ways military spouses can be a bridge between the military and civilians:

1) Be present.

Seek out local community events, not only military events, on post or on special occasions. Make an effort to talk to people outside of the military "bubble." When you live on or near a base that does a great job of building community on post, it can be hard to make the effort to reach those on the "outside," but working to integrate military and civilian life is important to challenging stereotypes. For a large majority of those serving, becoming a civilian one day is a very real possibility, so doing the leg work in order to stay connected to both sides will serve military spouses and their families as well.

2) Be transparent.

Let people get to know you and your family. Demystify the military family for them by talking about not only the lows, but the highs. Be open about what you enjoy about military life, the hard times, the lessons learned, and even what day-to-day life is really like. We have to be honest that, yes, deployments can be very challenging, but our spouses aren't always deployed. Talk about what the average day looks like for you and your family.

3) Give grace.

We can probably all recall things that have been said which showed a true lack of knowledge or understanding about military life. Even in moments like those, try to have grace. None of us say the right things all of the time, even to our military spouse friends. Give some extra grace to people who don't know much about the military when they occasionally put their foot in their mouth—at least they are trying!

4) Fall in love with each duty station.

This might be a major hurdle if you are stationed somewhere challenging, but find something to love about it. Get to know the best local BBQ, or hikes, or art museums, or live music spots. Remember, many of the civilians who live in the area chose that place to live, so there must be a good reason to like it. If you aren't sure, then do your homework and start asking around—we bet the locals will be more than happy to help you feel at home in your spot.

5) Take initiative.

If you meet a civilian and you seem to connect well, initiate planning to meet up or have them over sometime. They may assume that since your life is more unpredictable or different, you don't want civilian friends, and they may not make the first move. Be the one to extend a hand and show that you are interested in getting to know them more. We have a feeling they understand more than you know—after all, not every civilian has a 9-5 job, kids who never get sick, and hours to spend making new friends either.

We know it may not be the easiest or smoothest process to bridge the gap, but it is an important one for ourselves, our spouses and our country. The more we learn about one another and work together to overcome stereotypes, the stronger we are.

June: Summertime

Introduction

Summertime is always the best of what might be.
—Charles Bowden

    We hope you are in the midst of planning a road trip, some cat naps, pool days or just giving yourself some time off from worrying about life in general and embracing what long sunny days are for—relaxing!

    Summertime often gives us time to really enjoy our friends and family. The longer days allow for more time outside at the beach, park, lake, or a cozy campfire. We have more time to talk, give ourselves permission to eat ice cream, stay up later than usual, and maybe even get a sunburn. We encourage you to grab a friend (or your spouse if they are home) and do all the fun things that summertime allows. Make a list and make it happen!

JUNE: SUMMERTIME

Bucket List

Summer can fly by sometimes and we look back and wonder why we never made it to the beach, hosted that BBQ or checked out that awesome new waterfront restaurant. While we totally want you to sit back, we also want to be sure you get the fun stuff done! Here are some ideas for a summer bucket list.

- Go to the beach.
- Hike a beautiful new trail.
- Go to a drive-in movie.
- Read more books (maybe even visit your local library).
- Volunteer for a cause you all care about.
- Go camping.
- Finish (or start) a family photo album.
- Go to a Theme Park.
- Go to the Farmer's Market near your house.
- Visit the Zoo.
- Get ice cream from an ice cream truck.
- Go berry picking.
- Eat watermelon.
- Have a girls' night (even if it is just on Skype!)
- Take a dance or yoga class.
- Get a mani/pedi.
- Go on a weekend road trip.
- Send a package to a friend far away "just because."
- Go to an outdoor concert.
- Go to a delicious new restaurant.
- Plan your next girls' weekend.
- Play mini golf.
- Do something that scares you.
- Host a summer party.
- Get a massage.
- Go to a concert.
- Visit a winery/brewery.
- Go somewhere new.
- Take a class on something you've always wanted.
- Find a great new coffee shop.
- Invite friends over for brunch.
- Buy yourself something fun.
- PCS*—haha!

*All kidding aside, this time of year is usually seen as "PCS season" so this might be the only thing on your list, which is a pretty huge one if you ask us!

GOT YOUR SIX

Add some more things to your summer bucket list. Dream big...

JUNE: SUMMERTIME

Milspouse Summer MadLib

Remember these? Complete this MadLib on your own, with a friend, on a road trip or just sitting on the couch.

You know you are a military spouse when every summer you

_____ so this summer I will _____.
  (verb)   (verb)

I plan to take _____ and _____ (who are both
                (person)   (person)

really _____) with me to the _____ where we hope to
    (adjective)   (place)

_____ and _____. I don't even want to think
  (verb)   (verb)

about _____ and hope that nobody asks me to _____
      (verb)   (verb)

because it is _____.
             (adjective)

The one really _____ thing about my current duty
          (adjective)

station is _____ so I will be sure to _____ this
     (noun/adjective)   (verb)

time of year. I secretly really enjoy when I or my family go

on post for _____ because then _____.
       (place)   (phrase)

The one thing I hope happens this summer is _____,
                                    (verb)

because when it comes down to it, all that really matters to

me is _____.
     (phrase)

Summer Entertaining

Get out the twinkle lights and have a fun get together! It doesn't have to be expensive or fancy, just open the door and send out a text. Here are some party ideas and hosting tips we love:

- Host a BBQ (obviously!)
- Plan a "progressive meal" where you start at one person's home for appetizers, move to another's for the entrée, and end up somewhere else for dessert.
- Invite friends over for a themed brunch.
- Invite friends over for an "alphabet meal" where everyone brings a dish that starts with a designated letter ("P" for potato salad anyone?)
- Plan a popsicle and slip-and-slide party.
- If you have a backyard get a fire pit or chiminea for a late-night hangout.
- Get a projector and host an outside movie night.
- Plan a picnic.
- Host a taco party.
- Have an ice cream party.

Use the space below to plan a get-together this summer. Whether it's just a few friends or a huge gathering of neighbors, write down ways to make it special:

JUNE: SUMMERTIME

Don't Go It Alone

There's a flipside to the summer season that doesn't always feel so warm and sunny: those moments when it seems like everyone else is doing things together—except you.

Maybe you're the one in the national park parking lot trying to figure out how to strap on a toddler hiking carrier by yourself, or sitting alone on a beach towel while your kids play in the water, or standing awkwardly by yourself at a BBQ with a tight grip on your phone so you don't miss a call from overseas.

When these moments come, it can be hard to reach out to others. Maybe you don't want to intrude on your friends' special time with their families, because you know their service member will be gone soon enough too. Or maybe you just don't feel like answering the question, "How's your summer going?"

No matter the reason, we encourage you to continue to pursue sweet memory-making this summer, even when your spouse is gone and those memories won't look exactly the way you wanted.

What is holding you back from reaching out to friends this summer? How can you creatively get around those hold-ups?

Make a list of friends you can contact this month and events, outings, or activities you can invite them to. This could be anything from a simple stroller walk or park date, to a local weekend adventure or a girls' night out.

Food for Thought

Five Ways to be a Great Military Spouse Friend

We recognize that making a new military spouse friend can seem exhausting as you know at some point one of you will move—or, let's face it, fall off the grid for awhile following a deployment or gearing up for one.

But this same fact can be viewed as a positive—you will know people who live all around the world and you will have an ally when times get rough.

While it may be difficult to start yet another new friendship with a military spouse since you know you will be heartbroken when one of you moves, it is worth it.

Why?

Military spouses are fiercely loyal to their good friends. They are also amazing at maintaining relationships across the miles. We have made friends at each duty station and still keep up with them years later.

There are many ways to be a better friend in life, and as we know, military spouses appreciate the efforts as they are so often the "new one" in town or alone while their spouse is away for weeks and months at a time.

We know how it is to move somewhere new knowing you won't be there long and that "short timer's attitude" sneaks in. While it can seem tiring to take time to invest even when you'll only be there a short time, we know it is worth it. We encourage you not to give in to isolation and not to give up. Pursue friendship, even when it's hard, and life will be sweeter because of it.

We've shared five ways to be a better military spouse friend in the following pages. The ideas are not just for those welcoming a new spouse, but also between established military spouse friends.

Talk

Go knock on the door, give your new friend a phone call, Skype, Facebook message, etc. So often a military spouse is alone at home or alone with kids and talking to an adult will lift their spirits and help them stay grounded. Even if you don't have time for an in-person visit or a long coffee date, checking in with a quick text message to see how they're doing could mean the world to someone having a tough day.

Reach Out

Invite someone to coffee, cookies at your house, to go for a run, to a birthday party ... even a grocery store trip would be a welcome reprieve from isolation or loneliness. (There has been more than one occasion when walking around a Target or a PX has become a fun, friend building activity in our friendship.)

JUNE: SUMMERTIME

Ask the Hard Questions

Don't skip around the hard stuff. Ask how your friend is doing with a deployment, a difficult training or class, or a move. (Military spouses have learned to see through things anyway and will know if you are dancing around the hard stuff.) And if your friend tells you things have been hard lately, don't worry about fixing everything or saying the "right" thing—just be there to listen, laugh and maybe swing by later with a treat.

Surprise Them

A surprise package on someone's door step or tucked in their bag when they weren't looking will bring a huge smile to their face. So often the effort to physically give "care packages" is spent only on the spouse who is gone (which is well deserved, of course), but to have the spouse at home's sacrifice recognized with a personal gift can make all the difference.

Have Fun!

Through all the PCS moves, gearing up for deployment, going through deployment, welcoming a soldier home from deployment, changing orders, signing kids up for on-post care and more—we know your friends (and you) are in need of a laugh. Be sure to take time to keep things in perspective and if you have a friend struggling with seeing the bright side, make sure you help her out with a girls' night, pedicure, or Netflix night. Laughter is true medicine to the soul!

July: You're Sizzlin'

Introduction

It's a sure sign of summer when the chair gets up when you do.
—Walter Winch

This month is dedicated to the fact that you, sweet military spouse, are sizzlin'! It might sound silly but, let's be honest, sometimes we *need* this reminder.

In a world of impossible standards, yes, even in the military spouse community (maybe even more so sometimes with all the pressure we put on ourselves to be strong—can we get an Amen?!), we sometimes need to be reminded of how awesome we are. And in the true spirit of sisterhood, we need to remind each other!

Not quite sure you believe us yet? Read on to learn a few of the many reasons we think you're sizzlin' and see if your opinion changes.

JULY: YOU'RE SIZZLIN'

Baby, You're a Firework

Let's be honest because we are friends, okay? Summer is swimsuit season. How much do we tear ourselves down or hold ourselves back from enjoying that day at the pool, beach or lake by either not going at all, covering up so much that we aren't comfortable, or ruining what would have been a joyful day by comparing ourselves to everyone else?

Girl—stop, just stop! You are you—beautiful, wonderful, sizzling you! If you don't believe it, let us tell you why:

You are strong.

Physically, emotionally and mentally. Not just strong in the "go to the gym" or "you will just get through it" ways. Strong in the way that you keep pushing through, smiling, looking for a silver lining, and encouraging others to do the same.

You are wise.

Wise to the fact that things won't always be hard, or easy, for that matter. You enjoy both the sunshine and the shade, knowing you learn from both.

You can laugh at yourself (and appreciate others who do the same!).

How can we make it through life without the ability to laugh at ourselves? We think it's a crucial life skill!

You have a rockin' bod.

The kind of bod that totes kids around, cleans, cooks, walks the dog, pays the bills, studies and works hard.

You have a heart of gold.

The kind of heart that lifts up other military spouses, friends and family members who could use some love.

You are patient.

Patiently waiting for your spouse's return home, a change in scenery or a much-needed day off.

You are resilient.

You've lived far away from those you love, maybe even experienced a few deployments. You have PCS'd again and again, made a few new friends and said goodbye to old ones. You've quit jobs, gone back to school, and been frustrated with what feels like starting over again and again.

You are real.

You've seen good and bad times and you've walked beside friends who've gone through it all, because of this you can speak to others of the beauty and pain of real life.

You are a true friend.

You became friends with your neighbors or other spouses in your unit (maybe even to your surprise) and saying goodbye a year or two later was hard. But now you know the value of real friendship, so you've learned the art of maintaining meaningful, long distance relationships.

You can listen well.

Because you have been there! Now that you know what hard times look like you are more than happy to provide a listening ear when a friend walks down her own hard road.

You "speak" acronym.

PCS, ACU, TDY, ETS—you've got them down (or maybe not). But you know who to ask to translate, because let's be honest, the military life definitely has its own language sometimes.

You know how to do things on your own.

Brakes squeaking? Toilet clogged? Spider on the ceiling? You've got this, because you have to (even though you might not want to). You've done so many things on your own that when he comes home it can be hard to ask for help.

You support your significant other—even when it hurts.

There are many times when the career of our loved one calls them far away, or suddenly for training, or just long enough to not get separation pay (you know what we are talking about!). You did it anyway, though. You stayed strong and loving despite distance, fear and loneliness. It's hard, but it's worth it, so you persevere.

JULY: YOU'RE SIZZLIN'

Write down a few more ways you are sizzling! No one is peeking into this book, so it's okay to brag...

1.

2.

3.

4.

5.

GOT YOUR SIX

Guess Who Else is Sizzlin'?

Now that we've covered how awesome *you* are, let's turn our attention to the other sizzlin' hot military spouses around you. Here are a few ways to support another military sister:

- Invite someone over for coffee, dinner or dessert—socialize and have fun.
- Drop off a homemade treat.
- Invite someone new to hang out with you and your friends.
- Help a friend with kids, household items, or even a large project.
- Give your friend a compliment the next time you see them.
- Invite someone to the movies to beat the heat.
- Encourage your friend to take a date night with her significant other (offer to babysit for free that night.)
- Teach someone a new skill for free (baking, photography, etc.)
- Listen to a friend who is in a season of loneliness or hardship.
- Help a friend achieve one of her goals.
- Call someone you haven't spoken to in a while.

What are some more ways you can encourage someone? Who do you know that could use encouragement?

JULY: YOU'RE SIZZLIN'

Turn it Around

We think you're totally amazing. But you probably have a list a mile long of all the ways you fall short, don't you? Well, we disagree, but for the moment, let's set that aside.

We believe every mistake, struggle, and shortcoming can be used for good if we let it. So how can you turn yours around for good?

Maybe you think you're too introverted to thrive in this military life, where you're constantly forced to make new friends at the next duty station. Turn it around: you're a good listener and a loyal friend. You have a lot to offer to new friends at your next duty station, even if it may take a while to make them.

Insecurity/flaw:

Turn it around:

Insecurity/flaw:

Turn it around:

Insecurity/flaw:

Turn it around:

Insecurity/flaw:

Turn it around:

Friendship and Freedom

One of the hardest things about military life is that you're constantly saying goodbye to your best friend—your spouse. After all, you got married because you wanted to be around them as much as possible. Then, hello, military life! Turns out you'll be spending a lot more time apart than you ever expected.

Now you have a choice: stew in resentment and frustration because you don't get to enjoy the sweet moments with your spouse that you expected to have, or find a way to make the most of it in your current season. (You can probably guess which one we think you should choose.)

Here are some of the ways we've worked on friendship with our spouses during trips, deployments, and other hard seasons in the military:

- Reading a book together and exchanging emails about it.
- Texting daily or weekly about little things or life updates even when we won't get a chance to talk on the phone or Skype.
- Sharing funny photos, blog posts, and memes via email or message.
- Recording videos for each other.
- Planning a special trip or event for when they get home (sometimes planning together is half the fun!)

Make your own list. What are some ways you can deepen your friendship with your spouse?

JULY: YOU'RE SIZZLIN'

Let Freedom Ring

This month, we are celebrating America's Independence Day. We have all heard the phrase "freedom isn't free" and the saying rings so true to us as military spouses. We live such incredibly free lives in the US that so many others still long for—even still die for.

When you think of freedom, what images and ideas come to mind? What role do you feel soldiers and their families play in helping others be free?

Imagine if you lived in a country where freedom was barely even an idea. How different would your life be? How can you bring more compassion to your life today in light of the freedom that you do enjoy?

August: Celebrate

Introduction

When you wish upon a star ...
—Pinocchio

Take a moment to reflect. What have you done recently that you are proud of—something worth celebrating? What about a person—who, in your life, have you celebrated? We are talking about the kind of celebration where you dedicate time, an event, a dinner, a party simply to just to celebrate. If you haven't done this lately, you should, because your successes (big and small) are worth celebrating.

We are military spouses ourselves and love when other military spouses support each other in their hopes, fears and dreams. So in the month of August, we are focusing on the celebration of military spouses.

AUGUST: CELEBRATE

Who is a Military Spouse?

It could not be truer to say that there is no "one size fits all" when it comes to military spouses. We are teachers, doctors, entrepreneurs, sales agents, musicians, artists, runners, yogis, travel addicts, coupon clippers, coffee drinkers, shoppers, wives, daughters, sisters, mamas, work from home, work at home, work on the home, let someone else clean the house, Pinterest pinners, social media gurus or even anti-social media, dreamers and doers. Yes, definitely doers. If you want something done, call a military spouse—seriously!

We encourage you to stand tall and be proud of the milspouse you are. And don't let stereotypes, fears or deployments stand in the way!

When you think of the term "military spouse" what comes to mind? Has this idea changed and if so, why and how?

When you think of the most amazing "military spouse" in your life, who do you think of? What makes them so awesome?

GOT YOUR SIX

Worth Wishing

In 2016, we started The Six Box, a company that helps friends and family of military spouses send "reverse" care packages to the spouse holding down the fort at home during deployments. This little company came into being during a time of craziness, to be honest—deployment looming, stressful jobs, becoming first time parents, and more. But even though we were surrounded by stressful dynamics, we held onto our desire to help other military spouses and their marriages, and to let other military spouses know they are not alone. We have learned a ton along the way and are beyond thankful we decided to go for our dream together.

We think you should do the same!

What dreams did you have before becoming a military spouse that you felt you had to give up?

Brainstorm creative ways to get those dreams back—even if they won't look exactly the way you had originally pictured.

What have you accomplished so far this year that you are proud of? Big or small, write them all down.

AUGUST: CELEBRATE

Plan It

Now that we have reminded ourselves of all the things and people we want to celebrate, let's do it!

Here are some ideas to get you started on ways to celebrate:

- Host a "Friendsgiving".
- Drop a handwritten note in the mail.
- Host a celebration party, cake and all!
- Host a half year birthday party for someone you love.
- Have friends over for a themed dinner party.
- Send an unexpected present to your friend.
- Plan a girls' weekend.
- Make reservations at a restaurant you have always wanted to go to.
- Book a massage.
- Send a note of thanks to anyone who helped you along the way.
- Go dancing and invite others to join you.

Commit to it—what are you going to do? Write down the specifics of your celebration here:

GOT YOUR SIX

Pep Talk

In case you struggled with the first part, here's a little motivation from Wonder Woman, which essentially describes military spouses (right?!)

*You are stronger
than you believe,*

*You have greater powers
than you know*

—Antiope, Wonder Woman

Do you *believe* you are strong? What evidence do you see in your life that proves your strength?

If you struggle to believe you are strong, are there any lies you've been believing that are making it harder to see yourself clearly? Write down the lies, and the truth that you can lean on to oppose each lie:

AUGUST: CELEBRATE

Wishing on a Star

A dear friend of ours has a great family saying: "Find a need and fill it."

Maybe you don't have a dream right now, but you want one. Maybe you aren't sure where to start. We totally get it and encourage you to take your time and don't limit yourself. The smallest thing can be exactly what the world—or maybe even just your family—needs.

Here is some practical advice on how to find a dream:
- Ask people who know you what you are good at.
- Remember what you wanted to be when you were little? Sometimes, the answer can be found in your five-year-old dreams.
- Try some new projects, volunteer efforts, or types of work to see if you like something different than your current focus.
- Consider the jobs you have held in the past and what you did or didn't like about them.
- Read up on people who inspire you to see how they came about their careers or goals.
- Take a few weeks to keep a journal of your activities, likes and dislikes to see if a pattern emerges.

Use the space below to make notes as you get to know yourself and your dreams more this month:

GOT YOUR SIX

Pass it On

Do you have a friend who is working hard to pursue a specific dream? Can you come alongside her and help her achieve her goals?

Write down some specific ways that you will encourage or help her this month, and check them off as you do them:

Maybe you and your dreaming friend can even find a way to encourage each other, whether it's weekly coffee dates, monthly goal setting sessions, or annual skype dates to share the latest in your lives and celebrate one another.

Brainstorm some specific ideas for mutual encouragement below:

AUGUST: CELEBRATE

Food for Thought

6 Military Spouses You Should Celebrate

Why should the service members have all the fun, right? They certainly deserve all the ceremonies, but we think military spouses should be celebrated too.

Here are kinds of six military spouses we think you should celebrate. (We recognize this doesn't cover everyone, but have a feeling we can all relate to most of them.)

The Dreamer

The one who doesn't let a PCS, deployment, or less-than-desirable new home stop her from pursing her dreams.

She stays up late studying, researches all the ways she can maximize military spouse benefits, keeps a goal list taped to her wall, has a 5-year plan, and most likely wakes up early pursuing her go-getter life. She might seem intimidating, but truly she is inspiring and there is a wave of milspouses out there just like her changing the world. Celebrate this girl's ambition and resilience in the face of all military life can throw at her!

The Giver

Her husband, kids, neighbors, FRG members, extended family and more know she has their back.

She makes awesome care packages, including sending treats to everyone deployed (not just her man), does special events with her kids, makes her neighbor dinner, watches her friend's kids, and the list goes on and on. If there is a need, she is first to jump in and try to fill it. She has a heart of gold and genuinely loves giving to others. Celebrate her, because she is so busy running around filling up other people's cups that she probably doesn't even realize she needs a fill-up of her own.

The Do-er

She not only crosses off things on her checklist, she has multiple lists and still gets it all done.

She amazes everyone with her energy and ability to get so much done in 24 hours (or less). She is a coffee-filled wonder, bouncing from activities to planning meetings to PTA meetings and more. Sure, you can start to feel a little behind once you check in with her, but really, she thrives on getting stuff done—it's just who she is. This milspouse could use some celebrating so she knows all she is running around doing isn't going unnoticed.

The Chill One

We all need one of these milspouses in our corner—the one who doesn't freak out about anything.

Spiders in the house, broken cars, deployment rumors, contagious viruses going around at school—nothing phases this chick. She is the calm voice of reason we so often need when it literally feels like the world is falling apart. Celebrate this girl, because hey, she probably won't ever ask for it, but she will still think it's cool.

The Skeptic

After a couple years of military life, it can be easy finding yourself relating to this one.

Rumors of deployment, orders changing at the last minute, field exercises lasting longer than planned, and the other many changes military life can throw at us make it easy to question everything. It can be nice to have a military spouse friend around who questions the validity of every piece of info coming down the pipeline. One of the reasons she is skeptical is most likely because she has lived it already and has learned not to lean too much into news until it is really happening. We can call her the "voice of reason." She deserves to be celebrated for her willingness to question things many of us get all worked up about.

The "Average" One

In a crazy world full of comparison, multi-tasking, and my-welcome-home-outfit-is-hotter-than-yours, the "average" milspouse is what you need.

We can all relate to her, because let's face it, most of us are her. Average is good, people! She works out sometimes, can cook okay meals, attends some meetings (mostly running a few minutes late), maybe doesn't always get to her husband's Skype calls (because life happens), and enjoys eating cookie dough and drinking red wine on Thursday nights for no apparent reason (umm, don't tell us we are the only ones?). She's just awesome at being average and we all need to celebrate the friends who remind us that average is normal and okay. We don't have to be superwomen to live good lives!

We are probably all a mix of these six ladies, or maybe find ourselves gravitating towards one or two a little more than the others. We are so thankful for all the military spouses we have in our lives helping us keep things in perspective and not take ourselves too seriously.

At the end of the day, we believe all military spouses deserve to be celebrated—for the times when we are rocking it, the times when we can't see the light at the end of the tunnel, and then the "average" days too.

September: At Ease

Introduction

Great acts are made up of small deeds.
—Lao Tzu

    We see you standing there, worrying about going back to school, running kids to the doctor before sports seasons start up, planning for holidays, wondering how long it will take to settle into your new duty station and feeling the anxiety of carrying it on your shoulders. You are not alone. It is so important to remember that—there are thousands of women doing the same worry dance as you right now!
    This crazy month of September, when you start to wonder what happened to summer and how are Pumpkin Spice Lattes already on the menu, we want you to focus on simplifying and resting.
    Make it a priority to take mini breaks when you need them—schedule some "you" time.
    We've included a few tips and ways to stay organized and get back on track when it feels like the wheels are coming off. We want you to be the best version of yourself. And that starts with making sure you get the rest you need and without overcommitting or overextending yourself.

Over It

Have you come to the end of your PCS and are just *over* the endless unpacking, figuring out where to grocery shop, who will cut your hair now, and if you even like this new place? Maybe deployment is taking its toll—long nights, not enough communication and worrying enough for both of you?

While there are those obvious times in military life you might be over it, what about the days you are simply unsure about your spouse's career choice? The changing orders, constant moves, deployments looming, rumors of deployment—let's stop right there for a moment, because is there anything worse than your husband saying, "We think this will happen" or "Rumors are …" Whoa buddy, stop right there. We have too much on our minds to deal with "rumors" on top of it all.

What are things in your life causing you stress this month? Write them down and get them *out*.

SEPTEMBER: AT EASE

Take a Breather

We know we say this a lot, but we think you deserve a break—a moment, hour, day or two to just let it all go. Fall is just around the corner and life seems to speed up even more during this time of year. We are busy prepping for school, busy work seasons, upcoming holidays and more. So take a short step back. Now is the time to build weekly moments into your routine to allow for relaxation.

When you think about what really refreshes you, what is it? It might be a Netflix binge, but that also might just be an escape, and not a *true* source of refreshment.

Think deep, when was the last time you felt like your "cup was full" and what do you think the cause was?

Here are some of the ways we feel refreshed. Maybe one or two of them stands out to you:

Get out of the house

This is even more crucial when all you want to do is sit on the couch and wallow. Get out the front door and walk around your neighborhood, local downtown, park, waterfront, even the mall.

Take a bubble bath

It might sound too simple, but there are benefits to even a ten-minute soak. If you do a quick Google search you will see benefits pop up like: the steam is good for breathing, and warm baths can help with inflammation, soothe your skin and ultimately help you sleep better. An easy and budget-friendly way you can relax weekly, maybe even daily!

Meditate or Pray

Starting the day off in peace and quiet before the craziness begins is a great way to set the tone of the day. If this means waking up a few minutes earlier or finding time in the car to be quiet, it's important to take time to be still.

Phone a friend

A real friend—the kind you can speak unfiltered to. The kind of friend who knows something is up even if you don't come right out and say it. Those friends are pretty hard to come by so be sure to hang on tight *and* turn to them when you need a safe space.

Read

Reading can help us both escape the moment and teach us something new. Perhaps we will learn something that helps us right where we are.

Limit your screen time

The bright light on the computer, phone, or TV is so enticing and easy to get lost in sometimes, but it's not often that we feel truly refreshed by it. Set limits for yourself on how long and when you will use your devices (i.e. not at 12:00am when you are trying to sleep), and stop following people on social media who stress you out rather than helping you relax or building you up.

Count your blessings

Take time to write down or at least mentally count all the big and little things you are thankful for.

What else would you add? What can help you refresh in the midst of stress this September and beyond?

Which specific things will you do to take a break this month? Write down your restful activity, day, and time below, and don't budge when it seems like you're "too busy" for rest.

SEPTEMBER: AT EASE

Stress Less

We can't completely take away all the stress and worry, and all the warm baths and good books in the world won't heal the pressures of life completely. But we can help manage, plan for, and survive it. Here are some of our favorite strategies to plan for life's stressful seasons:

Journal

Cliché sounding maybe, but writing down thoughts is therapeutic and a safe way to express how you really feel. Sometimes when we write things down our perspective changes too and we find ourselves with a new attitude.

Plan

A simple white board or chalk calendar on a wall is a visual reminder to you and your family of what is coming up. If there is something you really want to do, put it on the calendar. Don't leave the good stuff to chance or hope someone reads your mind.

Meal Plan

Yes, you've heard it again and again, but it helps. When 3:00pm on Wednesday hits and you start hankering for a snack, you will be so happy you prepped. We even write down a menu on our chalkboard walls at home so the whole family knows what dinner is each night.

Drink less caffeine

This one is hard for us, because usually we enjoy a delicious cup of coffee as a way to "relax", but science has proven that more caffeine means more anxiety, so cut back a bit and chug some H2O.

Move

Seriously, no matter how stressful life gets, we all have 10-30 minutes a day to walk around the block, stretch at our desks or just lie flat on the floor allowing our body to totally relax. Set a reminder on your phone each day and make it happen!

Give to others

Sometimes we get so worked up in our lives we forget to notice that someone else is either going through the same thing, or something even harder. Look outward and not inward to see what those around you might need. In the end, you will feel better knowing you made a difference and you will have gained an ally in your struggle too.

Which of stress-management strategies will you adopt this month, and what new ones would you add?

SEPTEMBER: AT EASE

Help a Sister Out

Do you see another military spouse friend who could use a little breather? Maybe it's time you take turns serving each other—make a double batch of dinner one night, do a child swap, invite her over for wine and cookies, plan a day to the beach together. We aren't in this alone and it is important to remind ourselves of this fact, and to remind our friends, neighbors and even maybe someone you just met at the commissary.

Find a friend who would enjoy a little breather with you and make a plan—maybe even make it a regular thing! Perhaps you even do different activities with different people. This might fill up your calendar faster than you planned, so it's ok to go slow or cut back when you need to.

Make a list of friends you could help and a list of people you would enjoy hanging out with too:

GOT YOUR SIX

End the Tyranny of the Urgent

We often begin each day with a mile-long to-do list, but by the end of the day, only complete a small chunk of tasks. Which ones? Usually, the ones that feel most "urgent." We reply to that co-worker's email, return that phone call, and clean up the toys (because we just can't stand another minute in a chaotic living room—see, it's urgent!)

The tasks that get left *un*done tell a different story. They weren't urgent, but maybe they were important—important to our long-term goals, our sanity, our relationships, or our dreams.

Part of building rest and good planning into your life means ending the tyranny of the urgent—refusing to let small, seemingly-urgent tasks dominate your schedule, and instead making time to tackle the big, important ones first.

After all, social media, texts, and emails can wait. (The chores can wait too. Take it from us—they aren't going anywhere.)

But no one else can pursue your dreams for you, and no one else can rest on your behalf. Those two crucial "tasks" are completely up to you.

What urgent yet unimportant tasks do you find distract you, and what can you do to spend less time on them? For example, limit social media to certain time slots, or only reply to emails for a few minutes every morning and evening.

SEPTEMBER: AT EASE

What important yet long-term/non-time-sensitive tasks have you noticed that you tend to neglect? Write down each task, and then a specific time slot you can set aside this month to devote to each one.

GOT YOUR SIX

Food for Thought

Say Yes to the Best

As sweet summer comes to an end, it can feel kind of nice to get back to our normal productive routines, don't you think?

We break out our lists, charts, and planners with gusto. We sign our kids up for activities and take those adorable first day of school photos. We make meal plans and vow to prep healthy, home-cooked dinners every week—for real this time.

But in the whirlwind of productivity and planning, we often miss a crucial step: planning for rest.

Because rest isn't just about taking an annual summer vacation (let's be honest ... it was actually more of a "trip.")

Rest isn't something we do once a year when the weather is nice. Rest is—*should* be—something we intentionally build in to our weekly and daily rhythms of life. Rest is how we refresh, recharge, and renew, so that we actually have the energy we need to deal with the crazy things this military life throws at us on a regular basis.

"I don't have time to rest!"

We know. We get it. We don't feel like we have time either. That's why we picked this theme for September, after all!

Life for a military spouse never slows down. You're either gearing up for your service member to be gone, they are gone, you're preparing for them to come home, or you're dealing with that weird, "welcome-back-to-family-life-please-help-with-the-dishes" period known as "reintegration." Oh, and then there's the next trip already looming on the horizon, just in case you started to relax.

When you're dealing with all the responsibilities of "adulting" on top of the stress the military can take on your marriage and family, you don't have time to rest. And yet, in our experience, it's in these stressful seasons that rest is even more important than ever.

"Just make time"

The painful truth is that we only have 24 hours in a day, and yes, you do have to actually be asleep for some of them. Military spouses are pretty good at doing the impossible, but even we don't know how we're supposed to "make time" for rest.

When faced with the limits on what we can accomplish and how hard we can push ourselves each day, we have a choice: either embrace the limits, or pretend they don't exist—and end up getting burned out, miserable, and disappointed with life.

SEPTEMBER: AT EASE

We prefer embracing those limits. When we acknowledge that we can't get everything done, we are freed up to say "no" to the things that aren't essential, so that we have time and energy for the things that matter most—for our long-term goals, for our families, for our dreams, and yes, even time for rest.

Say "no" to good things so you can say "yes" to the best things

What counts as "good" versus "best" may change frequently, maybe even daily or weekly. The important thing is that you proactively choose what you're going to say "yes" to and what you're going to say "no" to, and you make sure that your commitment/workload allows ample time for the rest you need on a regular basis.

Need some examples?

Here are some of the things we try to say "no" to so that we have time and energy to do other things:

False rest

When you have an hour to yourself in the evening, what do you turn to? If you're anything like us, you probably turn on Netflix and open up a social media app on your phone. The next thing you know, the hour has flown by, it's past time for bed, and you feel more exhausted than ever.

TV binge-ing feels like it will be restful ("I just need to turn my brain off!"), but often it is simply a way to shut out the noise of life, not to actually refresh our souls.

And don't get us started on the tailspin of comparison, insecurity, and anxiety that an hour of social media can cause!

Instead, we are working on saying "no" to false rest, and using our free evenings for activities that we find truly renew us instead. For us, that can mean creative projects, reading, journaling or connecting with the people we love.

What forms of false rest distract you, and what do you find truly restful?

Perfectionism

"The best is the enemy of the good." —*Voltaire*

Relentless pursuit of perfection can drive us to spend way too much time on things that don't matter, leaving us with no time for the more important tasks—or to get any rest, for that matter.

Does your living room need to be spotless, or tidy? Does that blog post need to be a masterpiece, or is it good enough as is? Do you need a gourmet dinner each evening, or are a few nights of leftovers ok? Can you—*gasp*—even repeat the same meals every week and still enjoy them?

If you're stumped with a task or area of life that seems to take way too much time, try applying the Pareto principle. Ask yourself: How can I accomplish 80% of the same results while doing 20% of the work? The answer may surprise you...

People pleasing

You probably don't need us to tell you that a life of people pleasing will slowly drive you insane. But knowing it's a bad idea, and actually stopping? Those are two very different things.

When you make your plan for the month, week, or day, if part of your schedule seems a bit overwhelming, it might be a good idea to step back and ask, "Why am I doing this?" Why are you taking on that project, task, or event? Is it because you've decided it's more important to you than anything else you might do with that time? Or is it because someone else wants you to do it, and you care more about what they think than what you are truly called to do?

This is a tricky one because people pleasing may lead you to some very good things, like volunteering, serving others, spending quality time, showing hospitality, and doing favors. But if those good things get done while the best things languish week after week, that's a problem.

And the only solution to that problem is a kind smile and a polite "No." Or "Nope." Or "Can't, sorry!" Or maybe "Wish I could, but I'll have to pass."

Practice those powerful, freeing words as much as you need, then go get 'em, friend! You've got things to do, books to read, wine to drink, and bubble baths to take …

October: Contentment

Introduction

Many people lose the small joys in the hope for the big happiness.
—Pearl S. Buck

We wrote this month with you in mind—the planning, doing, being-all-things-to-everyone military spouse.

Oh, how we know you are striving to hold it all together and make it look good! You are in the throes of back to school for yourself, your kiddos, maybe even both. You are planning holidays and balancing your family and his, all the while hoping it all turns out okay. You are working to create the perfect Halloween costume, Thanksgiving feast, and holiday traditions, and most likely you are doing it on your own.

We feel you sister. We hear your mind planning and worrying over how you will get it all done and done well. We are right there with you and we know you are doing your best. We encourage you to try and be content with where you are. There is only so much you can do, and you only have so much control.

Time to stop worrying about being perfect and rest in contentment instead. Do what you can, but then sit back and enjoy the fruits of your labor—squeeze your kiddos instead of telling them to do more, have a glass of wine with your girlfriends on a Saturday afternoon instead of cleaning the house, and hey—just let your mother-in-law plan the Thanksgiving meal.

GOT YOUR SIX

What Can You Live Without?

As the busy holiday season approaches, we encourage you to seek ways to enjoy where you are and what you have. Maybe that means you make Halloween costumes by hand this year, or maybe you just buy cheap ones. Perhaps you don't worry about the perfect family photo, or you are okay with just trying a new exercise class instead of beating yourself up for not hitting all your fitness goals. Maybe you sleep in one day each week instead of frantically chasing a never-ending to do list.

Use the space below to list some things you can let go of in order to live with more contentment this month.

OCTOBER: CONTENTMENT

What Needs to Change?

When was the last time you did something without fear of judgement?

Want to have friends over without worrying about how your house looks? Try something new without having to be the best at it? Help your kid with a project without criticizing or wondering what other moms might be doing?

These shifts may seem small, but they help you build a habit of inviting contentment in. If you are worried about failing yourself, be honest about why these things are important to you.

Make a list of specific aspects of your life where you'd like to invite contentment in. Even if it seems impossible that it will ever change, put it on the list!

My Biggest Fears Right Now

You might find it odd to think about contentment with fear, but they often go hand in hand. We strive to change or improve things or maybe even avoid dealing with issues because we are actually afraid of where they stand or might be headed.

Think about reasons you might be trying to change or control relationships or situations, and write down what really scares you about them:

Relationship with my spouse:

Relationship between myself and family at home:

My emotions:

My health:

My finances:

My future:

My parenting plans:

OCTOBER: CONTENTMENT

What I Know is True

You've been bravely honest about your fears, but we don't want to leave you there. We don't want to live lives controlled by fear!

Use the space below to discover truths to lean on—to write out what is good about the same relationships and situations just as they are.

Relationship with my spouse:

Relationship between myself and family at home:

My emotions:

My health:

My finances:

My future:

My parenting plans:

What Are You Grateful For?

One of the greatest tools to combat fear and anxiety is focusing on gratefulness for what you already have.

Maybe you just enjoying walking around the mall and viewing the beautiful store fronts, or finding a free farmer's market to explore, or even (don't judge us for saying it) enjoying a Pumpkin Spice Latte. Write it down—even if it seems silly!

Use the space below to write what you are thankful for and come back here often, especially on the days you are comparing, striving and pushing for "perfect." If you put some people on this list, why not take some time this month to let them know you are grateful for them?

OCTOBER: CONTENTMENT

Food for Thought

5 Ways to be Content with Yourself

I (Megan) have always struggled with "accepting" myself as "good enough." I've struggled with constant feelings that have surfaced of not being "enough" while at the same time being "too much." As an adult with years of life experiences, friendships and lessons learned I can say without a doubt that most women I meet experience this paradox to some degree. In fact, two women wrote a book on this exact issue a couple years ago: *Wild and Free: A Hope-Filled Anthem for the Woman Who Feels She is Both Too Much and Never Enough.*

Isn't it sad that we are always judging ourselves so harshly? Do you ever wonder what we might be missing out on by not just accepting "me for me?"

I became a military spouse in my mid-twenties. The military lifestyle was a shock to my system. Suddenly, the government was telling me when to jump and how high. I had to start over in a new place every couple years or even months, you're always the "new girl," and you're living life on your own without your husband for long stretches of time. It all really tested my confidence.

It's hard (and let's be honest, sometimes exhausting) putting yourself out there and making new friends. Will they accept me? Am I too sarcastic? Too boring? Too loud? Too much of a military spouse? Not enough of a military spouse—so much that people think I don't get it or like this life at all? Am I crazy because I am a full-time working mom? Am I losing touch with friends and family miles away as we struggle to make a new "home" in faraway places? Am I too needy or am I being too strong? How long do I have before we have to start this process over?

Many times, I wanted to stay inside my house and not put myself out there. But I refused to do so (well, most of the time).

Although it is hard, I believe deep down inside that embracing myself as I am and putting one step in front of the other is actually the better, safer option. Even if it means sometimes I am a little too sarcastic or my house is a mess or I don't feel like I have anything to offer. I promise you right now I won't always say the right thing, do the right thing, be the best wife, mother, friend, daughter, cook, runner, etc. But occasionally I will nail them all!

Accepting yourself is a process and it looks different for everyone and happens at different times for everyone. I think it is unique to have the chance as a military spouse to meet people at different stages in their journeys. The friends I made at the start of this journey are still my friends and we have become parents and thirty-year-old somethings together. We've even become seasoned at saying hello and goodbye to our husbands together. The young women we were at the start aren't the same women we see today and we had the privilege to see each other grow through it all.

How grateful I am for friends who extend grace to me and how wonderful it is when I extend this grace back.

I'm slowly learning and implementing ways to accept myself. In the moments where I really disappoint myself, I try to remember five truths that I can always come back to.

I can only change so much

Honestly, there are only so many attributes I can change. I will always be almost 5'1"—I have been wearing the same size shoe since the third grade. I have gone through times when I liked being short and times when I didn't. But you know what? I can't change it and I have come to embrace that it is just part of who I am. I don't always remember important dates, I don't come from a perfect family, I am not always patient and calm, I am not the best at my job, my house isn't always clean and I am scared of public speaking. But you know what?

I can't do it all, and I can't be all things to all people. And I now know I shouldn't even be trying to do that.

I can only do my best with where I am and what I have been given. And to be truthful, I don't always do my "best" all the time—does anyone, really?

I was made for a reason and have a specific influence where I am

Cliché, but so true. The longer I am alive the more I see how my interactions with family, friends, co-workers, and neighbors have taught me things and allowed me opportunities to give that are aligned with exactly who I am.

There have been seasons where friends have given to me more than I have given back, and vice versa. I know people who challenge what I believe and hopefully others that I have been able to influence similarly with what I have learned.

Each time my husband and I have been apart we have learned to appreciate the friends and family who have stepped in to help us out during the separation. We've come to learn the value of digging into the community around us. The time living apart has allowed us to appreciate new people we might not have been hanging out with if we were living together. We currently live in an incredible neighborhood with military neighbors who will stop by with food, offer to walk our dog, ask if I need help with my kiddo, and more every time my husband is gone. I haven't truly experienced that in a military community before and it has been incredible.

It can be hard for me to accept help without feeling guilty, but since moving here I have learned to let go and just let people help. I do try to return the favor too!

OCTOBER: CONTENTMENT

Accepting myself enables me to love better

Have you ever been around someone who just shines? A confident, cheerful woman who is more concerned about others than herself? When I come across people like this, I am so drawn to them. Admittedly, they can sometimes appear to have it all together at first glance, but it doesn't take long to realize they don't, and the awesome thing is, they are fine with that. Looking at different times in my life when I have been more confident, I notice a trend—the less time I spend worrying about my faults, insecurities and what others think, the more time and room I have in my heart to love on others. Waiting on becoming the "right person" will only keep you from being you, from loving others with an open heart, and isn't that what we really want anyway?

Know you will change

The person you are today will most likely not be exactly the same in 5-10 years. Sure, a lot of who you are will stay the same, but the thing is, you can't go through life without being impacted by people and events. You will learn new things, be challenged by good and bad events in your life, have friends show you new ways of thinking and maybe even just put in the hard work to change something in your life you have always wanted to change. It is rare to come across someone who is exactly the same person they were in high school or college. So keep moving forward without constantly looking over your shoulder, second guessing who you are.

Comparison is the thief of joy, after all. Don't compare your middle to someone else's end!

You are awesome

It's true! You are incredible. There is no one out there like you. You are perfectly placed to be the friend, daughter, wife, mother, cousin, granddaughter, neighbor, co-worker that you are. When we hold back and constantly compare or worry that we aren't good enough we end up holding back our best selves.

Let's work together to accept who we are right now. Forgive ourselves for the past, remember we aren't perfect (and perfect people are boring anyway), and learn to move forward being our awesome selves right now, knowing that we will grow and change as life goes on.

When I look at my daughter, I want to teach her to accept herself for who she is, knowing she is unique, not perfect, and that is okay. The best way to teach her this is to live it—oh, what an incredible challenge that is!

I hope this month you have enjoyed working through cultivating contentment with us, because it is something we have to *work* on in this life. Give yourself some grace today and share it with others.

November: Thankful for You

Introduction

You are my favorite hello and hardest goodbye.
—Cecelia Ahern

As we rush into November, we wanted to send some thankfulness your way. So many people are thankful for you—so many more people than you know! And we are thankful for you too.

Thank you, awesome military spouse—thank you so much for all that you do. We want you to know your hard work and self-sacrificing acts of love do not go unseen. You are incredibly valuable to your family and your community. Those around you may not always say the words "thank you" but trust us, they are grateful for you.

NOVEMBER: THANKFUL FOR YOU

10 Reasons Why I Am Amazing

You read that right. You are amazing, whether you always feel like it or not. We encourage you to take a few moments and right down ten things that make you amazing. Do you rock at waking up early and getting stuff done? Do you make delicious cookies for care packages? Can you PCS and set up house in a matter of days? Are you the one person who remembers to send a card on everyone's birthday? Do you lead the FRG like it's a Fortune 500 company?

Write ten reasons why you're amazing:

1.

2.

3.

4.

5.

6.

7.

8.

9.

10.

How Can You Show Your Gratitude?

In this season of thankfulness, we want to show support to one another, especially as we reflect on how often other military spouses have reached out to us. No doubt you've given a lot to the military community and other military families you know. But you've probably also received a lot from other military spouses too.

Brainstorm ways you can show your appreciation to the military spouses who have gone above and beyond for you. Watching someone's kids, having a few spouses over for coffee and cupcakes, helping a friend clean the house or sharing a meal are simple but meaningful ways to express thankfulness.

This month, how can you show your gratitude to military spouses who have supported you over the years?

NOVEMBER: THANKFUL FOR YOU

In His Words

We polled our military friends to find some of the reasons service members are grateful for their spouse. Here's what these awesome guys said (awww!):

"I joined the Army for a couple of reasons, the first was to serve my country and the second was live the adventure with my best friend, my wife."

"The only reason why I can do my job overseas during deployment is because I know my wife if holding down the fort at home."

"I know that everything at home is being taken care of. Because of her I don't have to worry about anything but getting back to her."

"The tougher job is staying home. She works, takes care of our child, takes care of the home and bills. She doesn't get a minute off. I on the other hand am on a vacation compared to what she is doing."

"My wife is my rock who understands and supports me."

"I love her because she lovingly takes care of my infant son, takes care of me, and tirelessly supports our family."

"My wife is the glue that holds our family together."

"It takes an incredibly strong woman to manage a family when the father is at war."

"I have been amazed at the strength and resiliency my wife has displayed during our time in the military. She is my rock."

"There is no one who deserves more credit for the success of our family while we've been in the military. She's the backbone and lifeblood."

"Throughout all the time I've spent away from my family, I've never once questioned their wellbeing. My wife has always had my back."

Ask your service member why they're grateful for you, and be prepared for your heart to melt! Write down their response here and return to it often:

Your Love Story

Since this month includes a very special holiday where we honor our veterans, we wanted to encourage you to thank your service member and remember what made you fall in love in the first place. Write your story down from the beginning—first look, first time you met, first date, first anniversary, first child, even hard things like your first heartbreak as couple, first deployment, and more. Remember how special and unique you are to one another and make sure to express your gratitude through a card, care package, Skype, or if you are a lucky one, an actual in-person date night!

Write your love story here:

NOVEMBER: THANKFUL FOR YOU

Don't Brush It Off

When was the last time someone thanked you for something big? What was your response? If you're anything like us, you probably brushed it off. "It was nothing," "Oh, I was already going to do this other thing, so it was on the way," or "It was the least I could do."

It can be hard to receive thanks from others. Even when we know deep down that we *have* gone above and beyond and done something really special, we try to minimize the act. Why are we so quick to push ourselves to be grateful to others, but when others want to thank us, we freeze up and can't quite accept it?

Receiving thanks doesn't mean you're prideful or selfish. Sometimes, receiving thanks just means giving the other person the chance to "repay" you with all they have to offer—heartfelt words and a hug. Don't they deserve that chance?

Other times, receiving thanks can be like an intentional act of celebrating something good. You had more money, time, energy, or resources than you needed, so you shared it with someone else in need. To receive thanks for that act is simply to celebrate that you had something good in your life and were given the chance to share it. There's nothing wrong with that!

Do you struggle to receive thanks? How do you want to change in the way you respond when someone thanks you?

Food for Thought

7 Ways to Cultivate Contentment

It seems like just when things are going well, we try to hold onto them and then they fall apart, and then just when we can't take the hard times any longer, they change and get better, for awhile at least.

But we don't want to live on a rollercoaster. We want to be content in every season with whatever we have.

Sometimes that means being content with plenty rather than fearing that it'll all be taken away and wondering what we'll do if we lose it.

Other times it means being content with little, instead of comparing ourselves to other people and wanting what they have, or thinking that we'll finally be happy once we have more.

As military spouses, we go through such frequent—often radical—life changes. We're constantly tempted to live for the next season—the homecoming, the promotion, the new duty station, or even waiting for retirement, when "things will finally get better."

But the reality is every new season brings new challenges. A great new duty station that's in a place everyone wants to live might also have a higher cost of living, meaning you'll have to change your lifestyle accordingly. Getting out of the military means transitioning out of a tight-knit community into the wide-open world of civilian life, with all the changes and risks that entails.

Yes, there are hard things about being a military spouse, but there are also good things. And we want to be content as military spouses, even in the midst of all the chaos and challenges.

But what does contentment really mean?

Does being content mean being passive? Does it mean letting go even if things are not okay and just trying to be happy even though deep down you know you're falling apart? We don't think so!

Contentment doesn't mean that you don't make every effort to change your circumstances, to change what you really can control. It just means acknowledging that there are always going to be some things you can't control, or some things you have to sacrifice for other, more necessary things.

Contentment means resolving to seek joy and be satisfied, even when things are far from perfect.

It doesn't mean you don't work hard or seek improvement; it just means that in the midst of all that hard work and progress, you are content with where you are today.

In other words, it's a balance.

But what can you practically do to be more content beyond just saying the word "contentment?"

NOVEMBER: THANKFUL FOR YOU

Because that's what it really comes down to. We can say the words all we want, but unless our lives truly change, it doesn't mean much, right? So to answer that last question, here are seven ways that we've discovered to cultivate contentment even in the rollercoaster of military life.

Look for the opportunities within the hardships.

Yes, this deployment sucks, but hasn't it been a great opportunity to get to know your neighbors more? Or know the other spouses in your unit? Hasn't it been fun to hold the occasional girls' night, or spread out diagonally across the bed with no one to complain? You can finally live out your dream of being a blanket hog!

In every hardship, there are bound to be some opportunities. Seeing the opportunities in hardships isn't as simple as putting on delusional rose-colored glasses. No, it's a paradigm shift.

It helps us to go beyond feeling like victims of our circumstances, instead turning us into entrepreneurs who are able to generate profit from every difficulty, no matter how hard it is.

Record your lessons learned.

You don't have to keep a journal, but there's something about writing things down that really does make a difference in how you process them. It helps you remember more and it puts your brain in a different, more learning-oriented mode.

Recording lessons learned is a way to take control over a situation that has knocked us flat on our back.

We can't promise that we will make every decision perfectly and will never make mistakes in this life. Especially when things are changing so constantly and half the time we're just trying to keep up and survive. But we *can* look back and record lessons learned for the future.

For example, let's say you've just gone through a very busy season and you got burnt out because you over-committed and said "yes" to everyone.

Rather than thinking, "I hate how stressed I am, I wish my kids were older so I could do more," or "I wish my husband were here more so I could do all the things that I want to do without it being so overwhelming," instead, find a way to learn from it so that you can be more content in the future even if nothing really changes (yet).

For example, "I need to start saying no if someone asks for a favor that's not an emergency." Or, "I can't volunteer my time unless it's less than X hours per month."

Whatever it is, defining your lessons learned helps you to be grateful for the experience of learning a lesson and to be more proactive in making the most of the current season without waste or regrets. And even if it is a hard and stressful season, if you're proactive in learning from each thing that happens, it won't be a wasted season.

"We love each other, and that's what matters."

Relationships are hard—hard for everyone, and hard in every season, and not just for military families. But contentment in your relationships ... wouldn't that be a game changer?

No relationship is perfect, and no person is perfect. But we keep going back to that phrase over and over: "We love each other and that's what matters."

We don't have to agree about everything. We can have sharp disagreements about politics, religion, lifestyle, and parenting. We don't have to like each other all the time, or spend all of our time together, or share all the same hobbies and social circles. But we love each other and that's what matters. And often, that's all we really need.

Make the most of right now, knowing it won't always be this way.

It is so easy to always think about what will happen next—the next season, the next duty station. But this current season has its own benefits, and they won't always be available.

For example, when our husbands are in the field or working late nights, sure, we'd prefer to have them here and spend time together in the evening. But those quiet nights alone are great times to get work done, think creatively, or do things that normally we wouldn't do when we have them around. And we know it won't always be this way, so we try to take advantage of it.

Keep a gratitude journal.

This works for the simple reason that forcing yourself to come up with things that you're grateful for is an incredibly effective way for you to realize just how good your life is right now.

You most likely have access to clean water, good healthcare, a roof over your head when it's stormy, and heat when it's cold outside. You have plenty of food in your fridge and pantry. You have friends and family that care about you and would do anything for you.

Let's not underestimate what incredible gifts those are!

And it's easy to say, "Oh yeah, I'm grateful for this or that."

But when you take time to write it down and then review again and again, you force yourself to cultivate contentment a little bit more.

Make time for something special, just for you, every day.

This one is so close to our hearts. We're all about the importance of finding a little something special to enjoy every day. It doesn't have to be a cupcake. It doesn't have to be a new show on TV. (But it could be either—no judgment.)

The important thing is that every day you think of one thing that would be something special for you to enjoy and you take the time to do it.

That way, rather than neglecting yourself and feeling like an embittered martyr at the end of the day, you'll feel privileged, cared for, and loved—which you are.

NOVEMBER: THANKFUL FOR YOU

Sometimes for us, that's just a quiet cup of coffee before everyone else is awake so we can finish the whole thing without it getting cold. Other times, it's working on a creative project that doesn't have anything to do with business. Or maybe it's watching an episode of The New Girl or reading a few chapters in a good book.

For you it might be something different, like an amazing workout that gets you sweating, or a long walk with a friend, or maybe just texting with a friend who always makes you laugh. Whatever it is, take the time to do something special for yourself every day.

It's hard not to be content when you get to enjoy the good things in life every single day!

Notice the beauty around you.

Take a drive to see fall leaves, enjoy the scenic route if you have time, grab a bouquet of fresh flowers to put on your dining room table at home.

These might sound silly and small, but we believe beauty is a part of life. It's everywhere. And if we don't take time to notice and appreciate it, we're only robbing ourselves.

December: All I Want

Introduction

Leave a little sparkle wherever you go.

Because we love you, we want you to have that iconic Mariah Carey song stuck in your head just like we do this season:

> *I just want you for my own*
> *More than you could ever know*
> *Make my wish come true oh*
> *All I want for Christmas is you*

Sing it! Ooooh baby! Now that we're all singing the same tune, let's take a moment to be serious: the holidays can be bittersweet for military families. Maybe you've spent too many holidays without your spouse thanks to deployments, or maybe you're celebrating far away from your family because the military has called you to a distant new duty station yet again. When it comes down to it, if we really had to, we could do without the gifts and the cookies and the matching holiday outfits. All we really want for Christmas is that special someone under the mistletoe and the ones we love all within hugging distance. This month is all about those people we love, and finding ways to show we care, even—*especially*—when the holidays are hard.

Lovely military spouse, know that we see you and care about you immensely. Thank you for all that you do to serve our country behind the scenes. We are thinking of you and your family during the holidays this year and we truly hope that this month's topic goes a little way toward warming your heart.

DECEMBER: ALL I WANT

What Matters Most

The holiday season is often about people. Relationships. Stepping back from the whirlwind of everyday life to focus on what matters most to you. If you're going through a deployment this year during the holidays, that may feel painful, since the one who matters most is far away, and the holiday memories you long for might have to wait until next year. But we encourage you to write down what brings you joy anyway, even if it feels bittersweet.

Use the space to list the people, things` and experiences that matter most to you.

Holiday Memories

What are some of your most treasured holiday memories from the past? Write down a few of them here, and take a moment to savor the gift that these memories are to your life. Maybe it was opening presents on Christmas Eve with your family as a kid, or going sledding in the neighborhood, or shopping for gifts in stores that twinkle with holiday lights.

Write down those memories and treasure them!

DECEMBER: ALL I WANT

Do They Know?

Yes, it's the time of year when we focus on the people who matter most to us. But do they know how much they matter to you? Do they know that they would leave a big hole if they weren't in your life? What can you do to show them?

Use the space below to brainstorm ways to show extra love to the people you care about during the holidays. (This is so much more than gift giving!) Bonus points for creative ways to show a deployed service member or fellow military spouse how much they are loved during the holidays.

Love the Lonely

The holiday season can be bittersweet for a lot of people, not just for military families going through a deployment, but for anyone who feels like the message of holiday togetherness and joy only serves to highlight their own loneliness and hardship. Who do you know who is spending the holidays away from their family or just going through a hard time this year? It could be a fellow military spouse or a neighbor or a co-worker—anyone.

Brainstorm a list of people and think of some ways to show them they are not alone and not forgotten during the holidays. You could volunteer to feed the hungry one day during the holidays, or put together a care package for a neighbor, or simply write a little note for your friend and slip it in her purse. Be military spouse Santa this year!

DECEMBER: ALL I WANT

Your Wish List

Remember when you were a kid and you would spend weeks agonizing over the gifts you planned to request for Christmas? Funny how when you grow up, it becomes harder and harder to think of "what you want" when someone randomly happens to ask you. (Maybe because that's so rare—ha!) But having a wish list doesn't have to be a childish thing. It's about admitting your desires and refusing to give up on your dreams.

Use the space below to write your grown-up Christmas wish list. What do you really, truly want? Maybe it's simply to have him come home safely, or to have enough money to fly home for Christmas, or to finally get pregnant, or to reconcile with a distant friend. Or maybe it's a new pair of boots and some really nice lipstick. Write it all down!

GOT YOUR SIX

Letter to my Future Self

Can you believe the end of the year is already here? Before we know it, we'll be ringing in the New Year (or falling asleep on the couch while other, cooler people ring in the new year ... #momlife). We know you'll probably be coming up with a list of goals and/or resolutions for next year, or maybe simply a "word of the year." But before you jump in to goal setting, think big picture.

Use the space below to write a letter to your future self at the end of next year. What do you want to tell her? What do you hope she has done, felt, accomplished, or thought? Read this letter again at the end of next year.

DECEMBER: ALL I WANT

Food for Thought

Five Ways to Find and Keep Your Joy During the Holidays

This time of year just seems to put a magnifying glass on all of the anxiety and loneliness military relationships face. We know so many of you are doing the holidays alone for one reason or another, or this time of year is just hard for a myriad of other reasons. We encourage you to take it day by day and give yourself grace. This season is meant for joy, so we have suggested ways to help you find and keep your joy this season.

Trade Music for TV

Maybe this sounds too easy, but there are multiple studies on how music can lift your spirits. It can also motivate you (just think about those sweaty gym classes where they are blasting upbeat or rock music). Instead of going down the rabbit hole of mindless TV watching each night, try turning on your favorite playlist. You might just be inspired to do something fun, change your perspective on your situation, or just give your thoughts and emotions a chance to calm down a little. (It doesn't have to be Christmas music, either!)

Reach Out

This is arguably the easiest time of year to find a way to reach out to someone else. There are a plethora of organizations asking for both physical and monetary donations, help in a soup kitchen, sending a care package or more. But what about those closest to you? Your neighbor? Your family? Co-workers?

What if instead of just attending a party or giving a cutesy dollar gift from the Target One Spot Section (they *are* cute!), you really reached out? You could invite them over for dinner, or help a single mom (or mom with a deployed husband) with her kids. You could drive your elderly neighbor to the grocery store. You could sit with a wife who hasn't heard from her deployed husband in days and is beyond anxious. You could put anonymous notes and treats on the doorstep of the kids down the street. You could tell someone how beautiful you think they really are. You could take your kids somewhere they have been wanting to go just "because." You could sit down with your husband and ask him what he really needs from you.

You could devote yourself to the deep things, the real things in life—serving others in order to really help them where they are right now. We guarantee once you do this, your spirits cannot help but lift. And on the (selfish) plus side, we have no doubt they will want to return the favor somewhere down the road.

Simplify

Simplifying our house and life has become another goal on the list, a hashtag or an ideal to chase that few seem to truly ascribe to. While it is a hot topic and can be hard to do, we suggest you try this holiday season to focus on the basics. Don't try to do it all, be it all or have it all.

A good way to do this is to prioritize what really matters to you and put it in writing. Take the time to think about what you care about deep down this season and list things that pull you closer and things that push you away from these goals. Writing it out will help you be honest and make you more likely to stay accountable.

Savor the Good Things

Enjoy. Appreciate. Relish. Revel. Bask. Look around and try to enjoy where you are at, even if that means the Charlie Brown Tree in the corner.

Sometimes, joy is a choice, but it can be hard to choose. We have to fight for it and we understand we won't win the battle all the time. However, we encourage you to try looking at your situation with fresh eyes, or at least acknowledge that while this year is different, it doesn't mean every year will be.

Enjoy your warm house, food on the table, having someone you love so much you miss them, knowing you have a friend or family member that is a phone call away, an FRG that might just rock your socks off, a neighbor that looks out for you, or maybe the fact that you scored awesome presents during Black Friday or Cyber Monday.

No matter what the holidays look like for your family this year, you can still work to see the world from a place of joy. While we can sometimes feel the temptation to wish this time away, time is precious and we don't know what is around the corner. Taking time to bask in the here and now is so important.

Ask for Help

This may be the hardest one of all, because hey, we are military spouses. We can do it all (or most of it) on our own, and have been for months or years. We don't need help, right? News flash, you need help! Just admit it. Your friend messages and asks if she can drop off a treat, or your mom asks if she can help cook or clean, or your husband asks if you want something special for Christmas—say yes. If someone asks to help you, take them up on it.

This is still something we are both learning as we are pretty independent women. We can kill the spiders, do the cleaning, solo parent, hang the Christmas lights, help a friend out and more. But if we need something, we tend to push it to the back burner. We are learning that asking for help doesn't make you weak. In fact, it can even mean you are stronger and wiser because you're recognizing your limits and reaching out to someone who can step in. When you ask for help you let other people know you more, let them see you are human, and allow them to offer their skills and talent too—a win-win situation.

Afterword

One day, two military spouses (that would be us) got together over coffee. While chatting, we realized something worrisome: military spouses tend to take care of everyone around them. Their kids, their service member, their neighbors, that one friend going through a deployment, that other friend who just had a baby, and more.

But who takes care of military spouses while they're taking care of everyone else?

Like you, we want to see military marriages make it. One of the most powerful ways to ensure a marriage stays strong is to be sure both spouses are cared for. There are so many care package options and ways to support those who are serving overseas, but what about those standing beside the service member back home?

We started The Six Box because we wanted to do something practical to support military spouses, and through that, help military relationships survive and thrive through all stages of service. The Six Box offers a way for service members, family, and friends to send "reverse care packages" to military spouses going through a deployment or other hard seasons of military life.

This 12-month journal began as part of The Six Box, because we recognized that while snacks, hand-written notes, and pampering beauty products can be heartwarming treats, sometimes it is necessary to go deeper—to articulate our struggles and successes on paper, and to remind ourselves of the truth when we are bombarded by lies and confusion. We are now making the heart of our care packages available to anyone by offering all twelve months of the journal in one, easy-to-use book.

Check out our boxes for a military spouse in your life at TheSixBox.com.

Acknowledgements

Thank you to the incredible military spouses we know personally, the ones who have lifted us up in the hard times, inspired us in the good, and laughed with us at everything in between. Through the long nights, crazy days and constant change—you amaze us with your resilience, humility and tireless service to everyone around you.

Thanks also to our husbands, without whom we would never have known the joy of being military spouses in the first place. You are our forever heroes—thank you for your support, inspiration and unwavering service to your country and family.

And finally, thank you to our children. May our journeys inspire you the way becoming your mothers has inspired us.

About the Authors

Megan Casper and Alana Le are friends, neighbors, and military spouses with over ten years of military life between them.

As the wife of a first responder turned enlisted soldier, Megan became passionate about helping others develop skills that enable them to move through stress and transition with as much peace as possible. Megan is a mother, writer, and lover of organization, and believes almost everything can be fixed with a day by the ocean. Megan has a Bachelor's in Psychology from the University of Florida and is pursuing her certification as a Wellness & Life Skills Coaching Specialist from Auburn University.

Alana is a mother, entrepreneur, author, and lifelong laundry procrastinator. She never expected to marry into the military, but now that she has, she is so grateful for the tight-knit military community that has cared for her and encouraged her from day one. She has a Bachelor's in East Asian Studies from Davidson College and spent almost six years working in tech as an expat in Asia before moving back to the US to marry her real-life hero.

Made in the USA
Lexington, KY
07 April 2018